PREACHING

PREACHING

An
ESSENTIAL GUIDE

Ronald J. Allen

Abingdon Press
Nashville

PREACHING
AN ESSENTIAL GUIDE

Copyright © 2002 by Abingdon Press

This book is printed on acid-free, recycled, elemental-chlorine–free paper.

Library of Congress Cataloging-in-Publication Data

Allen, Ronald J. (Ronald James), 1949–
    Preaching : an essential guide / Ronald J. Allen.
        p. cm. — (Essential guides)
    ISBN 0-687-04516-9
    1. Preaching.   I. Title.   II. Essential guides (Nashville, Tenn.)
BV4211.3 .A43 2002
251—dc21   2002151826

Scripture quotations, unless otherwise indicated, are from the *New Revised Standard Version of the Bible,* copyright 1989, by the Division of Christian Education of the National Council of the Churches of Christ in the United States of America. Used by permission.

02 03 04 05 06 07 08 09 10 11—10 9 8 7 6 5 4 3 2 1

MANUFACTURED IN THE UNITED STATES OF AMERICA

To

Roger Guy (1933–2001)

Joann Guy

Robert Sutton, Sr.,

Ramona Sutton

who saw in me

more than I could see in myself,

and who,

in the tradition of the Christian Church (Disciples of Christ)

raised me up for the gospel ministry

Contents

INTRODUCTION

People who teach study skills say that when you read a book, you should take the following steps: begin by reviewing the book; flip through it to get a sense of the subject matter and the topics discussed; read the introduction to get the purpose of the book; most important, of course, read the book; subsequently, review what you have read, note questions that you have, and assess the strengths and weaknesses of the book; and, finally, discuss the book with others.

Readers can adapt these steps to each chapter in a book, too: overview the chapter; read it carefully; review it; and discuss it.

I hope that readers will follow these simple steps in approaching *Preaching: An Essential Guide*. This introduction facilitates this process by identifying the purposes of the book, and offering an overview.

The Purposes of This Book

This volume has two purposes. First, it provides a basic guide to putting together a sermon for persons who are new to this task. I write particularly for lay pastors and seminary students who are new to preaching, though experienced ministers can read the book as an update on current thinking about preaching.[1]

This volume is not a full-blown introduction to preaching. It is a handbook. People who complete this book may want to turn to the more comprehensive works listed in appendix D.

Second, this book provides a model for conducting a feedback session after a student sermon. In most preaching classes, students preach to their classmates and teachers. The class discusses each sermon with the preacher so that the preacher can identify (and build on) strengths and can name (and work on) weaknesses. The seven chapters in this book identify seven categories for such a discussion (described in appendix B).

The Approach of the Book

Most preaching books begin with a theory of preaching and then enumerate steps of sermon preparation. The reader follows a path from theory to sermon. This book takes a different route. It begins with a sample sermon (one of my own on Mark 9:49-50). In each of the seven chapters, I reflect on an aspect of sermon preparation or embodiment. The book thus moves from practice to the reasons and steps behind the practice.

I hope this approach will engage you and will remind you of the immediate practical value of methods of sermon preparation discussed in the book. I hope that beginning with a sermon will stimulate questions about how and why the preacher developed this particular sermon, as well as about preaching itself. I want you to ask, *How will I develop a sermon? And why?* The sample sermon is also a case study that I follow throughout the book.

Knowing that many readers want a summary of steps that preachers take in preparing a sermon, I provide such a sequence in appendix A.

An Overview of the Book

Chapter 1 reminds the preacher that the essential purpose of preaching is to bring good news from God to the congregation. Chapter 2 points out that the sermon should offer a clear message resulting from a disciplined encounter with a biblical text or topic. Chapter 3 develops three criteria to evaluate the situation of the congregation, the biblical text or topic, and the content of the sermon. Chapter 4 reflects on how the preacher and congregation can move from the meaning(s) of a biblical text or theological doctrine in the past to possible meaning(s) of such material for today. Chapter 5 stresses the importance of pastoral listening so that the preacher can develop a sermon that relates in a significant way to the congregation. Chapter 6 calls the preacher to develop the sermon so that the congregation can easily follow it. Chapter 7 provides practical suggestions for bringing the sermon to life in the pulpit in an engaging way.

I thank the members of the Writers' Group at Christian Theological Seminary who considered portions of the manuscript: Charles W. Allen, Wilma Ann Bailey, Brian Grant, Holly Hearon Felicity Kelcourse, Dan Moseley, Marti Steussy, Clark M. Williamson, and D. Newell Williams. Their comments enriched this book considerably. Where I have not followed their lead, I have put my work at risk.

"Have Salt Among Yourselves"

Mark 9:49-50

The text: "For everyone will be salted with fire. Salt is good; but if salt has lost its saltiness, how can you season it? Have salt [among] yourselves, and be at peace with one another." (Mark 9:49-50)

*P*reaching is never generic. It always takes place in a particular context. Context includes thoughts, feelings, actions, fears, hopes, and traditions that are at work in individuals, as well as in the communal life of the congregation and the larger world. Sensitive preachers relate the sermon specifically to the context in which it is preached.

I do not serve a local congregation. Since my ministry is centered in a seminary, I am typically a guest preacher in a local community. I developed the following sermon for a congregation of the Christian Church (Disciples of Christ) in Central Indiana when the pastor was away. The pastor asked me to preach on the text assigned by the Revised Common Lectionary for the day (on lectionary preaching, see appendix C).

Many people who participate in that congregation are discouraged because the congregation has been declining in membership for more than twenty years. Many members are weary from unrelieved institutional leadership. A few months before, the congregation had been involved in a public controversy when some neighborhood residents (not members of the congregation) objected that the congregation's food pantry and recycled clothing shop brought "undesirables" into the area. As guest preacher, I did not know enough about the particulars of the situation to speak specifically about them, but I did hope that the sermon could address the general discouragement that resulted from the congregation's public witness.

Sermon

"Everyone will be salted with fire." Now, that's a bracing image to begin a sermon: fire raining down like salt. Maybe, instead of distributing worship bulletins, we should distribute firefighter's hats. Instead of passing the bread and the cup, we could pass out fire extinguishers.

The two major images of this short passage are salt and fire. We usually think of salt as a seasoning that brings out the flavor in food. I was once in a Bible school class that was studying another passage about salt. The teacher had made vegetable soup and brought it to class in a big, old aluminum pot. The first activity in the class was to eat the soup: potatoes, carrots, green beans, tomatoes, corn, broccoli, okra, and even Brussels sprouts. But no salt. The class was polite enough, but as they ate, their faces showed the excitement of paint drying. Then, the teacher passed around a salt shaker, and the contrast between the unsalted and salted soup was such that one student cried out, "Move over, Julia Child. Our teacher is ready to go on camera."

To be sure, salt is not all good. It complicates high blood pressure. Too much salt makes you thirsty. But even so, we go for salt substitutes. Popcorn without the salt flavor is like no popcorn at all.

People in the world of the Bible valued salt as a flavoring. They also valued it for purifying and preserving. A spring was polluted outside of Jericho. Pregnant women who drank that water had miscarriages. The prophet Elisha threw salt into the water to purify it. After that, neither miscarriage nor death came from that water (2 Kings 2:19-22).

That would be a pretty good sermon: the church is to be salt in the world. It is to bring out the full flavors of life. It is to purify the water of life. But salt has an additional meaning.

In the Jewish tradition, salt became a symbol for covenant. A covenant is a promise between two parties. I promise certain things to you, and you promise certain things to me. In antiquity, parties often sealed a covenant by eating a meal that had been seasoned with salt. The salt represented their mutual promises (see, for example, Ezra 4:14).

In Judaism, the great covenant, of course, is the covenant between God and the community. When the Jewish people brought offerings to the altar for sacrifice, they rubbed them with salt.

Leviticus says, "You shall not omit from your grain offerings *the salt of the covenant with your God*; with all your offerings you shall offer salt" (Leviticus 2:13). The books of Numbers and Chronicles refer to the promises between God and the community as a "covenant of salt" (Numbers 18:19; 2 Chronicles 13:5).

I can imagine that each time the people tasted food seasoned with salt, it reminded them of the promises of God. "I am your God. You are my people. I am with you always. I love you with unconditional love. I desire justice for you and for all, and I will continue to work in the world until it comes."

The covenant includes life among people within the community, too. When the people cut covenant with God, by definition they cut covenant with one another to live together in love and justice.

So when Mark mentions salt, we think about God, and about God's promises to be faithful, and about our promises to witness faithfully for God.

But do you notice the association of salt with fire? "For everyone will be salted with fire." What is this being salted with fire?

I have a lot of positive associations with fire. Singing around the campfire at church camp. Cooking marshmallows for S'mores on the beach. With winter coming, I look forward to putting the logs in the fireplace, filling the house with the crackle of the fire, and pulling up the rocker, and just watching the fire burn.

But we have to set aside these happy feelings when we come to the fire in our passage. Mark, along with many others of his time, believed that the end of this world and the beginning of a new world was arriving soon, and that terrible times would come right before the end. They called this terrible period "the tribulation." They expected that, in the tribulation, faithful people would suffer because of their faithfulness. The unfaithful would resist the witness of the faithful, and would even do harm to them. The unfaithful would try to make things so hot for the faithful that the faithful would give up on God. Many people in Mark's day spoke of the tribulation as a time of fire.

I imagine few of us think about the tribulation in this way. But we do not have to believe that the end of the world is coming right away in order to appreciate Mark's message. Sometimes Christian life and witness is like being in a fire: you make your witness, but then other people resist, object, or even try to harm the Christian community.

15

The church to which Mark wrote was flaming (so to speak) on the outside and on the inside. In 70 CE the Romans burned the Temple, one of the most important symbols of Judaism (Mark 13:2). Where were the promises of God then?

The fire was burning on the inside of the church, too. The Markan disciples argued about who was the greatest in the church (Mark 9:33-37). Jerusalem was in flames, and they were arguing about who got to drive the fire truck. Then the disciples saw someone who was not in their church casting out demons and they tried to stop him (Mark 9:38). This exorcist was releasing people from the grip of Satan, and they whined, "You can't do this because you're not a member of our church." Where were their promises to one another as a covenantal community?

Sometimes life is a fire. Sometimes the fire is hot in the church. And sometimes it turns faith and witness to ashes.

It's easy to taste the salt, the promises, when life is young and beautiful. It's easy to taste the salt when a baby is born healthy and has not dirtied its first diaper. It's easy on a wedding day when the whole world seems blooming with flowers and love. It's easy when your congregation takes a stand on a controversial issue and everyone cheers.

But you feel the fire when that baby grows into a surly teenager who lives in a cave and comes out only to feed and growl, and you have to have tough love. It's hard when you wake up one morning, sixty years after the wedding, and look across the breakfast table, and realize that you cannot take care of that person by yourself any longer. You roll the person into the nursing home and leave him or her there in the stagnant smell of cleaning fluid and stale cigarette smoke. It's hard when your congregation takes a stand for the poor and the hungry and the homeless, and people picket your church and make snide remarks behind your back and confront you in the lunchroom.

"Salt is good," Mark says, "but if salt has lost its saltiness, how can you season it?" That is, when the fire gets hot, how do you keep going in faithfulness to God and one another? "Have salt among yourselves," that is, remember. Remember the promises of God. "Have salt [among] yourselves." Tell the promises of God to one another. Remember that God is always with you—every day, every moment, every breath. Even in the fire. *Especially* in the fire.

That's why we come to worship. To remember the covenant that

God has with us, and the covenant that we have with one another. To have salt among ourselves.

Before the breakup of apartheid in South Africa, our family spent a summer in Zambia, a nation just north of South Africa. We were at a school where students came from all over Africa to study. One day a chaplain came from a native African group in South Africa to visit the South African students at the school. Many of these students were exiled from their homeland because they had been involved in the struggle for freedom and justice. Some of them had not seen their families for a year, or five, or ten, or fifteen years.

Communication is so unreliable in that part of the world that some of them did not know whether friends or sisters or brothers or parents were still free or even alive. As one of them said, "Some days, the police come and take them away, and you never hear from them again." The chaplain had come with packages and news.

When I went around to greet the chaplain, I instinctively extended my right hand. But the chaplain met my right with a left. I looked down: he had no right hand. He was a leader in the struggle for freedom and justice. Some years before, a package came in the mail. When the string was pulled to open the package, it exploded, incinerating his right hand. Salted with fire.

We felt anguish for him and for the students. But anguish is not what I recall most. Even now, I see the flash in the chaplain's eyes. I feel the strength and warmth of that left hand. I see the chaplain tall and easy, leaning against the Land Rover. The chaplain and students make their way from under the giant shade trees down to the student houses where they laugh and talk into the night. They remember life in South Africa. And they remember the promises of God: "I will be with you. I love you with an unconditional love. I will work for justice until it comes."

They start singing. We lie in our beds and hear their voices coming through the forest. The rhythm. The beat. The fullness of the sound. After a while, they got into songs that the missionaries had taught them, and one of those songs brought a catch to my throat [*I speak the following words quietly and slowly in a way that suggests singing*]: "When through fiery trials your pathway shall lie, my grace, all sufficient, shall be your supply."[1]

"Have salt [among] yourselves." Remember. Remember the promises of God: "I am with you. I love you unconditionally. I am at work for justice in your world." Remember your promises to live in love with one another. Every time you taste salt. Remember.

In the chapters that follow, I return to this sermon for examples. I say more about the purpose of the sermon, why I interpret Mark 9:49-50 as I do, the context of the sermon, why I put the sermon together in this way, the illustrations, and how I embodied it.

As a next step in preparing for reading subsequent chapters, you might pause to reread (or listen to, or watch a tape of) a sermon that you have recently preached, and engage in the same exercises. While reading the book, you might reflect on your sermon, and ask, What would you do the same as when you preached it? What might you do differently, given the discussion in the book? *For your next sermon, how will your preparation and preaching be reinforced or changed as a result of your encounter with the ideas in this volume?*

If you are not preaching (and, perhaps, have never given a sermon), you might think of a sermon that you have recently heard as a case study to follow while reading. While reading the book, you might reflect on this sermon and ask, What did the preacher do that is consistent with the principles articulated in this book? What could the preacher have done differently that might have enhanced the sermon? *Given what you are learning about preaching, how might you preach your version of that sermon today?*

Many people who are new to the study of preaching begin to think about preaching from the perspectives of the sermons they have heard. Take a moment to think about the preaching you have heard over the years. Do these sermons and preachers influence the way you think about preaching now? I invite you to compare and contrast the way you think about preaching now with the ways your perspectives change as you work through this volume.

CHAPTER ONE

What Is the Good News from God in the Sermon?

At the beginning of a preaching class, I always ask the students, *What is the purpose of preaching?* The following responses (and others) always come up: "The purpose of the sermon is to help people deal with their problems." "Preaching should challenge Christians to live their faith." "The aim of the message is to convert people to Christianity." "The preacher should prophetically call for big changes in our society." "Sermons should motivate members to participate in church programs." Someone wisecracked, "The sermon gives worshipers a little nap during the service."[1]

While most of these responses contain measures of truth, none says quite enough, nor do any reach to the heart of the vocation of preaching. As the title of this chapter suggests, the basic purpose of preaching is to bring good news from God to the congregation.[2] In a sermon feedback session, the first question is, *In the sermon, what is the good news from God for the congregation?*

This chapter first describes why good news from God is the intent of the sermon. I stress the importance of the sermon being clear. The chapter then takes up the issue of where the preacher gets this good news, and concludes with a consideration of how God is active in all phases of the sermon—from preparation through preaching to aftereffects.

The Sermon Is Good News from God

The idea that Christian preaching is good news assumes that the world contains some bad news. A biblical name for this bad news is "sin." The Bible and Christian theology contain multiple definitions of sin. I will not get into the fine points that distinguish different understandings of sin, but most preachers would agree that sin is a condition in which individual human beings, social groups, and nature fail to reflect fully the purposes of God for all things to work together in love, mutual support, and abundance. This general broken condition is manifest in particular ways such as restlessness within the soul; jealousy and hostility in personal relationships; idolatry; racial injustice; gender discrimination; tribalism; economic exploitation; sickness; poverty; and violence.

The Bible and Christian theology assert that, through Israel and Jesus Christ, God testifies to the divine desire to repair the damage done by sin and to restore the human and natural worlds to their divinely inspired purposes. The sermon is good news because it helps the community recognize and respond to an aspect of God's renewing presence. The good news, in short, is the news, confirmed to the church through Jesus Christ, of the promise of God's unconditional love for each and all, and God's unremitting call for justice for each and all. The preacher interprets the situation of the congregation and its world from the perspective of this gospel.

The sermon is good news not only because it helps the congregation perceive that God is repairing the destructive work of sin, but also because God is constantly in the world to manifest love, justice and other forms of blessing. The preacher helps the congregation perceive ways that God seeks to intensify these good things.

By saying that the sermon is good news I do not mean the preacher ignores sin. Far from it. The preacher is called to name sin as well as the complicity of the congregation in it. Unless the preacher does so, many people will think that God intends the brokenness. Without such interpretation, people sometimes think that disappointment, brokenness, suffering, and exploitation are normal. However, a sermon should not stop with naming or even denouncing sin. For the gospel is the news that God is at work to regenerate the world.

Every semester a student asks, "Must *every single sermon* be good news?" I respond that messages should *typically* take the form of good news. Most sermons help the congregation understand the gospel, experience it by way of the language of the sermon, and determine how to live the gospel in the everyday world. However, I can imagine situations in which, to prompt the congregation toward a special moment of reflection or behavior, a pastor might preach a sermon that does not explicitly articulate the good news. For instance, in a community that has refused to think about an important issue, the pastor might preach a sermon whose goal is to provoke reflection. Such a sermon might actually intend to roil the waters of the congregation so that they will recognize the importance of the issue. However, in such circumstances, the preacher and worship leaders want to make certain that other parts of the service assure the congregation that God is for them in their struggle.

I recommend a little exercise for preachers to help them be sure that they are communicating good news from God in the congregation: summarize the main drift of the sermon in a single indicative sentence.[3] The subject of the sermon is God. The verb is an activity of God for the restoration of the world. Typically this activity is a demonstration of unconditional love, or an attempt to bring about justice. The predicate is the result of God's redeeming activity, and possibly, our response.

For the sample sermon, this sermon in a sentence is "God promises to be with us and support us even in tribulation (that is, when our witness to the reign of God brings us into conflict with others)." An implication is that we can engage in faithful witness even in tribulation because we know that God is in covenantal relationship with us. Other implications are also possible. For example, the motif of "having salt *[among] yourselves*" suggests the importance of being joined with others in Christian community.

This formula and the sentence that summarizes the sample sermon are as follows:

Subject of the Sentence	Verb	Predicate
God	Activity of God for the restoration of the world	Result of God's redeeming activity
God	Promises	to be with us and support us even in tribulation

21

By making God the subject of this sentence, and the subject of the sermon, preachers remind themselves and the congregation of the centrality of God in the Christian worldview, and of the fact that God's gracious initiatives make possible (and call forth) human response. Preachers often need to discuss what the church (and other persons and communities) need to do, but such human activity is always in response to possibilities from God.

The sermon in a sentence cannot summarize everything that the preacher wants to say. However, it is the central idea around which the sermon revolves. In the sermon itself, the preacher may amplify this leading motif, draw out its implications, compare and contrast it to other ways of thinking, and even question it.

Formulating the news of the sermon in a sentence helps preachers avoid two common mistakes: works righteousness and moralism. Works righteousness is the belief (sometimes unconscious) that human beings must do certain things, perform certain works, for God to love and accept them. For instance, a preacher may suggest that members of the congregation need to give a certain amount of money to the church in order for God to bless them. Moralism is reducing the Christian life to a set of behaviors. The moralistic preacher spends the sermon telling people how to live without showing that Christian life results from God's grace.

Preachers do need to discuss Christian works. Christians perform good works not to earn God's love, but to act out our identity as a community whom God loves unconditionally. We do not engage in faithful witness to earn God's love, but because we are loved.

The Sermon Needs to Be Clear

The congregation needs to have *a good opportunity to get the point* of the sermon. Notice the italicized words in the preceding sentence. While the preacher must make the sermon clear, the preacher cannot guarantee that the congregation will get the point. Factors that are not related to the sermon itself may cloud the congregation's reception. Parents may be preoccupied by their teenagers' Saturday night activities. A single woman may be considering the deposition she must make in the sexual harassment charges against her supervisor. A leading elder may have indigestion.

Many factors interfere with a congregation's actual ability to follow the sermon. However, the preacher is responsible for putting the sermon together so that it is clear enough that members of the congregation have *a good opportunity* to follow it.

Some preachers today think that the idea of a sermon having a "point" is outdated. The term "point," they say, implies that the sermon is like a lecture whose purpose is only to communicate intellectual content, whereas they insist that preaching should involve an emotional component. They say that the sermon is more an "experience" than the communication of a point.[4] Hearing a sermon is more like going to a good movie than attending math class. A movie does not directly state its message. Moviegoers enter into the world of the movie; the experience of following the plot creates the message of the movie. The attempt to state the point(s) of a good movie always oversimplifies the message of the movie and does not take full account of the experience of the movie itself.

To be sure, a sermon has experiential elements, and the statement of a "point" never fully explains the experience of hearing a sermon. For two reasons, however, I am convinced that preachers need to summarize the theological heart of the sermon in a single statement: (1) some people in the congregation are intellectually wired in such a way that they must hear the "point" in order to get it; and (2) by summarizing the gist of the sermon, the preacher is better able to evaluate the theology of the sermon (see chapter 3). You may think it strange that a whole subsection of a chapter is devoted to the importance of the sermon being clear. However, after twenty years of hearing multiple sermons every week in class, I can assure you that many preachers need this reminder. Every week I hear sermons that are simply random collections of pieces of information about the Bible, ideas, stories, and images. When the sermon is over, I feel confused, let down, and frustrated. When congregations have a similar experience week after week, when the sermon begins they soon tune their antennae to other channels.

Where Does the Preacher Get the Good News for the Sermon?

Much of the rest of this book helps one develop the sermon as an event of good news. I pause now to overview key elements in this process. Both here and in appendix A, I lay out these elements as if

23

they take place in the same sequence week after week. In actual practice, they sometimes occur in very different orders. Over time, preachers develop their own patterns of sermon preparation.

The preacher seeks to interpret the situation of the congregation from the perspective of the gospel and to help the congregation interpret the gospel from the perspective of its situation. Consequently, the pastor must have a clear and credible understanding of the gospel as well as a deep and sensitive pastoral understanding of the congregation, along with an adequate theological method for helping engage in this mutual interpretation.

In the broad sense, a minister formulates the good news for a particular Sunday, considering points at which the congregation needs to understand its life and the life of the world more fully from the standpoint of the gospel. The preacher must choose whether to engage in this interpretation with the help of a biblical text or by focusing on a topic. The difference between biblical (or expository preaching) and topical preaching is discussed in chapter 2. Many congregations follow the Christian Year and the Revised Common Lectionary as a basis for preaching (see appendix C). In such congregations, the preacher usually develops the sermon from one or more of the biblical texts that are assigned for the upcoming Sunday. However, congregations are not enslaved to the lectionary; preachers can choose other biblical texts or topics.

After a preacher has selected a text or topic, the preacher must come to a thorough understanding of it. If the preacher has decided to preach from a biblical text, a preacher carries out an exegesis, that is, a disciplined attempt to understand a text in its historical, literary, and theological contexts. At this point, the preacher is not drawing out what the text means for today, but is trying to determine what the passage meant to people in antiquity. If the preacher has decided to preach from a topic, the task is to study the topic in order to understand its origins and history, its current manifestation, and why it is important. The study stage is discussed in chapter 3.

After gathering a responsible understanding of claims of the text or the phenomenon of the topic, the preacher theologically analyzes the claims of the text or the phenomena surrounding the topic. I recommend using three foci for theological analysis. Is the text or topic (a) appropriate to the gospel? (b) intelligible? (c) morally plausible? (For these criteria, see chapter 3.)

When the preacher has made a cogent theological analysis of the text or topic, it is time to name the good news that is at the heart of the sermon. What does the preacher most want the congregation to hear concerning the subject of the sermon? At this point, I find it extremely helpful to formulate the sermon in a sentence. The preacher seeks to relate the interpretation of the sermon with the text (or topic) and the specific situation of the congregation. A preacher may amplify or extend the witness of the biblical text—usually through the hermeneutic of analogy—or topic. Or, a preacher may agree with aspects of a text or topic but disagree with others. In a few cases, a sermon may actually stand against a biblical text or a topic. Chapter 4 outlines the different relationships among preacher, congregation, text, topic, and direction of the sermon.

The preacher puts together the sermon as a whole. There is no single formula for arranging the various parts of the sermon. The preacher may draw on a stock sermon outline or may create a movement for the sermon. *Patterns of Preaching: A Sermon Sampler* contains thirty-four different approaches to putting the sermon together, and that number is only a small sample of various types.[5] These matters are discussed in chapter 6.

The preacher makes sure that the sermon fits the context of the congregation (see chapter 5). Toward this end, a sermon should contain at least one life-like story with which the congregation can identify that illustrates the good news of the sermon.

The pastor prepares to preach the sermon. Preachers need to be sure that the sermon is in their hearts and souls so that they embody the sermon with energy and passion (chapter 7).

Sermon preparation and the actual event of preaching have both conscious and intuitive elements. Most of the work of putting together a sermon and speaking it to life in the pulpit takes place at the conscious level. In fact, preachers make critically informed choices at key moments of preparation. However, preachers often find that intuition and other transconscious modes of perception play a role in preaching. Ideas and images can float into the preacher's awareness at any time of the day or night. I often find that my subconscious is at work on a sermon even when I am sleeping.

God Is Active in All Phases of the Sermon

The study of preaching contains a whole subject area called "theology of preaching," which is a theological interpretation of what happens in preaching.[6] It explains God's relationship to all phases of the conception and life of a sermon. It takes into account the characteristics of the listeners and how people perceive, the content of the sermon, the place accorded to Jesus Christ, the role of the sermon in God's activity in the world, the function of the Holy Spirit, and the place of the sermon in the congregation.

In such a short book, I cannot develop a whole theology of preaching. But I can suggest main lines in God's relationship with the sermon. God, through the Holy Spirit, is active in all phases of the sermon, from the formulation of the sermon to the congregation's response to the message. The idea that God is active in all aspects of the sermon is an extension of the Christian conviction that God is present at all times and places and is at work to lead everyone involved in a situation toward the divine purposes of unconditional love and justice.

God seeks for the sermon to help the community name, experience, and respond to these divine aims of love and justice in every heart and every relationship. At each stage of the genesis, maturation, and afterglow of the sermon, God hopes that the preacher, the congregation, and the larger world will come to as full a grasp as possible of the divine love and call for justice.

I do not believe that God has a blueprint for every sermon that the preacher needs only to discover. God made human beings to be creative as preachers and as listeners. The sermon is always an act of interpretation. But in ways that fit every situation, God desires for pastor and people to have optimum understandings and experiences of grace.

The idea that God is present in every situation does not mean that everything that happens in the process of preparing and preaching follows the divine leading. Sin distorts our capacity to understand or witness fully to God. Under the influence of sin, preachers and congregations can be self-serving, idolatrous, and exploitative. This finitude is why it is important for preachers to test their insights in the broader community to see, as 1 John says, whether they are of God. Both preacher and congregation need to be ready to evaluate their convictions and, if necessary, reformulate them.

When the preacher and congregation do not follow the divine invitation to witness to unconditional love and a community of justice for each and all, God does not abandon the situation. God works with the choices the people make to help them move as far as possible along the road toward love and justice. Even when we yield to sin, God seeks to help us recognize and respond positively to thoughts, feelings, and actions that can move us toward regeneration. As a colleague puts it, "One of the great things about God is that God never gives up on you."[7]

Following the suggestion at the end of the sample sermon (p. 18), think about your own sermon or about a sermon that you have recently heard that is your case study as you read this book. Try to put the main point of the sermon into a single indicative sentence. Is that point good news that helps the preacher or community name and respond to God's unconditional love and will for justice? If not, does the sermon drift toward works righteousness or moralism? How could you reformulate the main point, and the sermon itself, so that the message becomes an event of good news?

Chapter Two

Does the Sermon Honor the Integrity of the Bible or the Topic?

A preacher usually develops a sermon in one of two ways: as an exposition of the significance of a biblical text, or of a topic. The preacher needs to come to a full-bodied understanding of the possible meanings of a biblical text in its historical, literary, and theological contexts, or of the origin and manifestation of the topic.

A text or a topic has integrity in the same way that a person has integrity: I am who I am, and I have the right to be who I am; I am not who other people wish I would be.[1] Similarly, a text or a topic is what it is, and it is not simply a projection of what one wishes it would be. Preachers today sometimes refer to this quality as "otherness."[2] While the preacher is related to the text, it is other (different) than the preacher, and it deserves to be respected for what it is (and is not). Indeed, its differentness, its otherness, often prompts one to think about the world, God, and oneself in fresh and provocative ways. A key step in the preparation of the sermon is to relate to the text or the topic, as much as possible, as an other, and not just as an extension of one's values and wishes.

Consequently, a key question in sermon feedback is, *Does the sermon honor the integrity of the text or topic?* I want to help the preacher identify the degree to which the preacher has listened attentively to the text or topic in its own right, or has made the text or topic into the preacher's own image.

The chapter first considers factors that go into whether to choose an expository or topical approach. The main parts of the chapter outline basic steps in biblical exegesis and in coming to understand a topic.

Imagination can play an important role in this part of the preparation of the sermon. However, exegesis of a biblical text and interpretation of a topic involve considerable study for which there is no shortcut or substitute. The preacher simply has to get books off the shelf and turn some pages, or call up some information on the web, or turn to some journals. When this work is complete, the preacher is ready to analyze the theological and moral claims of the biblical passage or the theological and ethical assumptions of the topic in preparation for formulating the direction of the sermon proper.

Making the Choice: A Text or a Topic?

One of the early steps in sermon preparation is to choose whether to preach an expository or topical sermon. On what basis does the preacher decide? This choice is rooted in two things: the comparative strengths and weaknesses of preaching from a text or topic, and the situation of the congregation. The preacher selects an approach to the sermon in the hope it will correlate with congregational context.

I join most other people who teach preaching in believing that expository preaching should be the usual focus of parish preaching. The Bible has a proven record of helping the church discern the presence of the living God. The Bible contains stories and ideas that are foundational to Christian identity. The Bible introduces and explains much basic Christian language and many Christian practices. Even when the Bible does not directly consider an issue faced by today's church, it often offers situations that are analogous. Much of the language of the Bible is amplified and reshaped in later Christian theology; when we are in touch with their biblical roots, we develop an intuitive sense of their primal power. The Bible is not monolithic, but contains a pluralism of theological ideas and practices, thus offering today's pluralistic congregation many points of entry into the biblical world. The Bible is often a lens that helps us see God, the world, and ourselves more clearly. Furthermore, biblical and theological illiteracy are big problems in many congregations today; expository sermons help congregations become familiar with the content of the Bible and with how the Bible can help their growth in discipleship.

The sample sermon in the introduction, "Have Salt Among Yourselves," is an expository sermon. I try to hear Mark 9:49-50 in its setting in the world of Mark and to reflect on how that passage can illuminate the congregation today.

However, the Bible does not address all situations that congregations face today, nor does it contain the fullness of Christian doctrine that has matured over the centuries. Furthermore, the Bible contains some religious ideas and moral prescriptions that are theologically problematic. For such reasons, topical preaching can be a valuable supplement to biblical exposition. When preaching topically, the preacher starts with a topic that is important to the congregation. Topics may come from doctrine, theology, Christian practice or from personal or social issues. For example, a pastor might develop a topical sermon on the Holy Spirit, or providence, or prayer, or human sexuality, or racism.

The preacher has no simple formula to determine whether to develop an expository or topical sermon. Through pastoral listening to the community, the preacher must develop a deep knowledge of the congregation and a sense of the degree to which a congregation would likely benefit from an expository or topical message, and choose accordingly.

Identifying and Respecting the Otherness of a Biblical Text

The term "biblical exegesis" refers to the disciplined process of locating the possible meanings of a text in its historical, literary, and theological contexts. The term "exegesis" derives from two Greek words meaning "to lead out of." Through exegesis, the preacher intends to lead meaning out of the text so that we can identify it and relate with it. A goal is to identify and respect the otherness of the text; that is, the text as it is in its own right and not simply as a projection of the preacher's own theology, personal and social values, and ethical commitments.

We often speak of "eisegesis" as the opposite of exegesis. The designation "eisegesis" is made up of two Greek words that mean "to lead into." Pastor and congregation engage in eisegesis when they read their theologies and values into the text, regardless of whether these qualities are actually in the text.

Exegesis sometimes means that a preacher must admit that a text contains characters, actions, ideas, or images that seem very strange to contemporary people. In exegesis, the preacher does not ignore these things or interpret them away, but states them. We need to hear the text in its otherness. In a later stage of sermon preparation (chapter 3), you can analyze the text theologically to determine theological points at which the text challenges you and points at which you need to challenge the text.

When I was preparing the sample sermon "Have Salt Among Yourselves," I initially resisted the ideas that Mark expected the world to end very soon and that the time before the end would be a tribulation. I do not subscribe to either of those theological ideas. It would be easy for me to engage in eisegesis by reading my theology into the text. Instead, I forced myself to respect the otherness of the text. In the sermon proper I identify the claims of the text, and then indicate the points at which I, and many in the congregation, do not share the convictions of the text: "I imagine few of us think about the tribulation in this way. But we do not have to believe that the end of the world is coming right away in order to appreciate Mark's message."

Possibility of Multiple Interpretations

This discussion of exegesis must be nuanced. When I was in theological seminary in the 1970s, we often spoke of exegesis as determining *the* (singular) meaning of a text. We operated as if a text had only one objective meaning that could be identified by engaging the text by the various exegetical methodologies. Today, we speak not of *the* meaning of a text but of possible *meanings* (plural). We recognize that texts are open to multiple interpretations, depending upon the social location of the preacher, the exegetical methodologies used, and the interpretation of the data in the text and in its larger world. However, the possibility of a pluralism of meanings does not mean that any interpretation is legitimate. The preacher's interpretation of the text must be plausible from the standpoint of the text's historical, literary, and/or theological context.

The Preacher Must Be Self-aware

Before proceeding with exegesis per se, preachers should be aware of their social locations and of the biases that they bring to the act of interpreting the Bible. By social location, I mean the values and assumptions that accompany the preacher's class, race, gender, sexual orientation, political philosophy, theological position, and so forth. We tend to interpret texts exegetically and theologically in ways that support our social location. When we are not conscious and critical of our social locations, we can easily drift into eisegesis.

For instance, I am a middle-class, Anglo American, male, heterosexual who leans toward a socialist political philosophy, and am a Reformed theologian with an orientation toward process theology in the stream of revisionary theology. Hence, I tend to interpret texts in such a way as to support, and certainly not disturb, my comfortable middle-class lifestyle, and the social power and privileges that come with being Anglo American and male. I tend to find social communitarianism in the Bible, and I want to think that Moses was the first Reformed theologian and that the roots of process theology are in the Bible itself. I need always to be aware of ways in which I tend, often unconsciously, to interpret a text eisegetically to get it to support my social location and to disrupt me as little as possible.

Preachers need to be aware that social location can make one more sensitive to elements in a passage that are overlooked by conventional Anglo male preachers and scholars. Feminist interpreters criticize aspects of male privilege (patriarchy) and seek to find materials in the Bible that empower women for egalitarian relationships with men and that call for social relationships that are mutual and nonauthoritarian. Interpreters from racial and ethnic communities other than Anglo American are often especially alert to aspects of texts that Anglo American middle-class males (and others) have used to exploit and repress persons of color. Racial and ethnic preachers often hear messages of social and political liberation that do not occur to their Anglo American male counterparts.

Steps in Biblical Exegesis

There is no one method of biblical exegesis. In fact, biblical scholarship today speaks of more than a dozen methods of biblical interpretation. I outline a *basic* approach to interpreting the Bible that incorporates basic tenants of historical, literary, and theological methodologies.[3]

(1) What Are the Natural Starting and Ending Points of the Text?

The preacher must determine that the text on which the sermon is based has literary and thematic integrity. It should start at a natural point and end at a natural point; that is, a point at which the earlier passage ends and the succeeding passage begins. The text should be a meaningful unit.

A preacher usually should not preach from a single verse. Not only were verses and chapters not included in the original text of the Bible (they were added only in the tenth century), but a verse is seldom a meaningful unit. A minister who preaches on a single verse usually extracts that verse from its literary context. This procedure is usually eisegetical.

Even when a text is given by a lectionary, the preacher should look at the starting and ending points. The committees that assemble lectionaries sometimes begin and end the readings at arbitrary places that confuse the meaning of the text.

The sample sermon is based on Mark 9:49-50. Mark 9:40-48 is a distinct literary unit. Mark 10:1 begins a new section. Mark 9:49-50 is the conclusion of a series of passages that are thematically linked, beginning with Mark 9:30. I allude to the larger setting in the sermon.

(2) What Is the Historical Setting of the Passage, and What Is the Purpose of That Passage in That Context?

Many texts in the Bible were spoken or written to address a particular historical situation. When we know something about that situation, we can better understand the point(s) that a text was trying to make in that setting.

However, a preacher must sometimes distinguish between two historical settings. One is the setting that is described within the passage itself. For instance, in the book of Genesis, we hear stories of Abraham and Sarah, Isaac and Rebekah, as well as Jacob, Leah, Rachel, and Joseph. These characters lived about 1800 BCE. The preacher can investigate what we know about the actual historical settings of these characters, although the preacher may find that we do not possess a lot of firm information.

The other historical setting is the one for which the book of the Bible containing the text was given its present shape. The Gospel of Mark, on which the sample sermon is based, was written during a time of social and theological crisis. The Romans had destroyed the Temple (one of the primary symbols of Judaism and divine faithfulness); the church was in increasing tension with Judaism because it was receiving Gentiles into its community without converting them to Judaism; the internal life of the church was rent by jealousy, discouragement, and confusion over mission. In this milieu, the writer seeks to encourage the community to remain faithful and to engage in mission by calling attention to the belief that they were living in the last days and that Jesus would soon return in a cataclysmic apocalyptic event to end the present world and begin a new one. As noted in the sample sermon, this knowledge of the Markan situation allows me to hear Mark 9:49-50 with precision and depth.

I often find it helpful to imaginatively enter the world to which the text was written by asking questions derived from the five senses, to which I add a sixth sense. The preacher should answer these questions *as people would answer them in antiquity.* We need to be careful not to simply project our associations onto the text. We need to go to reference books and other sources for help.

- What do I see?
- What do I hear?
- What do I touch?
- What do I taste?
- What do I smell?
- What do I feel? That is, how does it feel to be a part of the world of this text?

We may not always have the data or methods to reconstruct the historical situation of a text with certainty and detail. In that case, a preacher may be able to surmise something of the general historical setting without getting into much detail. It appears, for instance, that much of the Wisdom Literature was written by middle- and upper-class people who sought to reinforce their relatively secure and comfortable ways of life (as in the Proverbs), or to explain and help the community live with interruptions to that life (Job). But, the preacher cannot be more specific.

How does the preacher determine the historical context of a book of the Bible? One can turn to the introductory sections of commentaries on books of the Bible that usually contain a segment on the setting, or to chapters in an introduction to the First or Second Testaments, or to articles in Bible dictionaries. The beginning preacher needs to be forewarned, however, that scholars sometimes interpret the setting in very different ways. Hence, the preacher must sometimes select the interpretation that makes the most sense.

(3) What Are the Meanings of the Key Words in the Passage?

The study of the words in a biblical text has a direct benefit for the sermon. When we know the meanings of its key words, our perception of a text often becomes deeper. The congregation is often fascinated by word studies.

In their contexts in the ancient world, words often evoke depth of significance and association. I have a simple rule in this regard: take nothing for granted. The preacher needs to inquire into *every* word in a passage: *How would listeners in antiquity have heard this word?* This rule is necessary because words often change meanings and associations over time, and a preacher can easily hear a word in the text along the lines that we might use it today without uncovering its ancient usage. The preacher needs to ask how to understand the words in the text from the standpoint of their use in antiquity.

For instance, relative to the world of ancient Judaism, translators often use the English term *law* to translate the Hebrew word *torah*. In contemporary North America, our associations with *law* are ambiguous. Many Christians think of the Jewish law as a set of legalisms that enforce works-righteousness. In the wider culture, the term *law* is often associated with legal requirements to restrict behavior, and with a complicated system of jurisprudence. In some corners, *law* is associated with narrow-mindedness and legalism. Late-night television comedians continually make fun of lawyers as ambulance chasers and profiteers. We do look upon the law system to guard civil rights and to maintain order in society, but even in these contexts the notion

35

of law evokes a certain sense of coercion. By contrast, the purpose of torah is to teach the community the ways of God and the pathway to blessing. To be sure, torah includes some statutes and regulations, but the basic meaning of *torah* is instruction that is regarded as a great gift. Indeed, the psalmists and others praise God for Torah. The preacher who hears the word *law* in the more restricted senses not only misses essential elements of *torah*, but misrepresents the essential meaning of *law/torah*.

In the sample sermon on Mark 9:49-50, word study revealed that Mark uses the term *salt* in a figurative way to speak of covenant. Mark uses the notion of fire to speak of the tribulation. Although the word *tribulation* does not appear in the passage, the passage presumes ideas contained in that notion.

How does the preacher find the meanings of specific words in a passage? The Bible dictionaries contain concise articles that trace meanings of the key words. When using a Bible dictionary, the preacher needs to be careful to look up how the word is used in the passage that is the focus of the sermon. A particular biblical writer or a particular passage sometimes gives a word a special meaning. Mark, for instance, uses *fire* and *salt* in distinctive ways in Mark 9:49-50. The Bible commentaries often discuss how key words are used in the passage under study. The preacher can use a concordance to look up occurrences of the word (and its cognates) in other passages. The concordance led me to the passages about salt that I cite in the sample sermon.

(4) How Does the Literary Context Help Us Understand the Passage?

One of the most familiar axioms of biblical interpretation is that a text apart from context is pretext. The preacher wants to know how literary context enriches our understanding of the passage. Literary context involves both the immediate setting (the material on either side of the passage) as well as the larger setting of the whole book (or other body of literature) in which the passage occurs.

With respect to *the immediate literary setting*, I find it helpful to ask three questions: (1) Does the material that comes prior to the text prepare the way for us to hear the text? If so, how? For instance, Mark 9:49-50 appears to have little immediate connection with its context. But the key phrase "Have salt [among] yourselves" suggests that

Mark intends to call the church into covenantal community. When we go back to Mark 9:30-48, we see the disciples thinking and acting in ways that violate covenantal faithfulness. This setting is integral to understanding 9:49-50. (2) What happens within the text itself as a part of that context? Mark 9:49-50 calls the congregation to recover qualities of covenant as the center of their common life. (3) Does the material that follows the text flow from it? If so, how does the text contribute to that flow? Mark 10:1 and the verses that follow do not depend heavily on Mark 9:49-50. However, the material that follows 9:49-50 does deal with aspects of covenantal life; for example, maintaining relationships between spouses (10:1-12), respecting all in the community (10:13-16), using material resources to provide for all in the community (10:17-31), disavowing power for one's own ends and using power for the sake of the community (10:32-45).

With respect to *the larger setting* of the passage, a preacher can ask, *How does the work as a whole enrich our understanding of the passage? Likewise, how does our understanding of the passage enrich our understanding of the larger work?* To respond to these questions the preacher needs to be familiar with the work as a whole.

One will often find that previous study of another passage or another part of the Bible provides information for interpreting the text at hand. I first encountered the motif of "tribulation" years ago in connection with another project. When I first turned to Mark 9:49-50, I did not anticipate finding echoes of tribulation. But as soon as I began to converse exegetically with the text, the tribulation theme became apparent. Indeed, the more I thought about tribulation and the Gospel of Mark, the more I realized that tribulation is a part of the whole ethos of the Gospel. Study has a long-term cash value.

Returning to Mark 9:49-50, I find few direct verbal links with other parts of the Second Gospel. For instance, the words *fire* and *salt* do not occur elsewhere in Mark in ways that illumine this passage.[4] However, the notion of the tribulation occurs several times in Mark, preeminently in 13:3-23. Although the latter passage is spoken in the future tense, most scholars think that it refers to events that were already happening in the Markan community.

(5) What Is the Literary Style and Function of the Passage?

In the last twenty years, the relationship between the literary style (often called form or genre) and function (or purpose) of a passage, and preaching from that passage has been a source of insight for many pastors. By way of analogy, the preacher is already aware that different kinds of material in the newspaper is written in different ways and has different functions. For example, front-page news stories, advertisements, cartoons, and editorials are all different in format and function. The reader expects a different kind of encounter from each kind of material.

Similarly, the Bible is made up of different kinds of material, each of which has its own literary style and function. Some of these genres can be quite extensive, while others can be quite brief. The story of Abraham and Sarah, for instance, is a saga—a narrative whose purpose is to reveal the identity of the community and to locate the community in time and space. A parable (a genre of literature) is relatively short and is usually designed to surprise the listener into thinking afresh about the subject of the parable. In the Gospel of Luke, the parable of the good Samaritan (Luke 10:25-37) prompts the listener not only to ask, "Who is my neighbor," but to recognize that persons against whom we are biased (represented by the Samaritan) can actually be agents of the divine will and providence, and can treat us as neighbors. This awareness causes us to rethink the way we usually categorize people and to open us to the great reunion of the human family that will take place in the reign of God.

The preacher, then, needs to ask two questions of each passage: (1) What is its literary genre? (2) What is the purpose of that genre?

The purpose of a text may suggest a similar purpose for a sermon. A saga, for instance, may suggest a sermon whose aim is to help the congregation rediscover its identity. A message on the parable of the good Samaritan could invite people in the contemporary setting to consider who functions for us in ways akin to the function of the figure of the Samaritan in the world of Luke.

This analysis was not as helpful with respect to Mark 9:49-50 as some other approaches to biblical interpretation. In form, this short passage is probably a chreia, that is, a statement from a significant character (Jesus) intended to influence the living of those who receive it. As noted, Mark 9:49-50 intends to motivate the community to recall the trustworthiness of God in the midst of end-time tribulation. I had already come to this insight by means of step 2.

While the investigation of the literary form of Mark 9:49-50 was not especially significant for the preparation of the sample sermon, this phenomenon illustrates the fact that the preacher will not find every method of biblical interpretation to be equally useful every week. Some weeks historically oriented approaches will be more suggestive, while other weeks literary approaches will be more promising.

The Bible commentaries usually tell the preacher the form or genre of the text. Sometimes the preacher needs to go to a Bible dictionary or a handbook of biblical criticism (interpretation) and look up an article on the appropriate genre (for example, saga, parable, proverb, or chreia).

(6) What Does the Passage Invite Its Listeners to Believe?

A text typically invites its readers to believe its claims about God, the world, and humankind. This step is not so much a fresh methodology of interpretation as it puts the theology of the text into an explicit summary. Contemporary people must decide the degree to which the claims of a biblical text are authoritative for them. We need to make a critical appraisal of the text. In chapter 3, I lay out an approach for doing so; but first, pastor and people need to have a clear view of the theological claims of the text.

I find it helpful to summarize the theological ideas of the text in terms of three questions. While I enumerate these questions separately, their themes intertwine. The preceding steps turned up information and perspectives that make it easy to respond to these questions in the case of Mark 9:49-50.

(a) What does the text ask us to believe about God and God's purposes for the church and the world? While God is not explicitly mentioned in Mark 9:49-50, foundational apocalyptic convictions underlie Mark's understanding of God. God is the sovereign of the universe. God either initiates or permits all things that happen. God wants all people, and all elements of nature, to live together in love and justice. The reference to salt calls to mind God's covenantal faithfulness to the promises that God has made through Jesus to the disciples. Although the text does not mention the Great Judgment directly, the reference to fire reminds the reader that, after the end of the present age, God will judge all people, welcoming the faithful into the divine reign and consigning the unfaithful to eternal punishment.

(b) What does the text ask us to believe about the world and God's

intention for it? As indicated earlier, Mark assumes that the world in its present form is ravaged by sin and must be reconstituted if it is to manifest the divine purposes fully. Through the life, death, resurrection of Jesus, God is intervening in the world to end the current era of history and to begin a new age (often referred to as the reign of God). God will complete the work of restoration after the return of Jesus. Mark believes that this return will take place soon and that, in anticipation, history has entered a phase called the tribulation, a time of suffering that comes about as Satan and the minions of evil entrench in opposition to God. Mark wants the church to recognize that suffering, caused by both external forces and internal conflicts, indicates that they live in the end times.

(c) How does the text invite listeners to respond to the divine presence in the world? What does the text claim that listeners should believe and do? The text invites the community to remember that God's faithfulness will carry them through the difficulties and suffering great tribulation, and that during that time the community is to continue to witness to the reign of God.

The main purpose of exegesis is to help the preacher and the congregation respect the text as an "other" and not too quickly to co-opt the text for the various agendas of the preacher and the congregation. The next phase in preparing an expository sermon is to make a theological analysis of the text to determine what the congregation can actually believe today about that text. Such a process is described in chapter 3.

Identifying and Respecting the Otherness of a Topic

Whereas the preparation of an expository sermon starts with the exegesis of a biblical text, the preparation of a topical sermon begins by identifying and investigating a topic.[5] Conduct an exegesis of the topic.

A topic is a Christian doctrine, a Christian practice, a personal or social issue that can be better addressed from the standpoint of the gospel than from the exposition of a biblical text. The following are examples of topics: the providence of God (a Christian doctrine), prayer (a Christian practice), choosing a life mission (personal issue), affirmative action as an issue of racial justice (social issue).

The goal of the topical sermon and the expository sermon is the same—to help the congregation encounter the gospel and interpret its life from the perspective of the gospel. A key element of reaching toward this goal is to come to understand the topic as an "other."

When would a preacher turn to a topical sermon? The expression "better addressed" in the preceding paragraph points the way. A topical approach can help the sermon get to the heart of a subject with more directness than by means of an expository sermon. Paul Scott Wilson, distinguished professor of preaching at the University of Toronto, believes that a preacher can get to any subject from any biblical text.[6] Wilson is probably correct. However, the route from text to subject is sometimes so circuitous that the preacher is advised to save the time necessary to construct that route and to go directly to the interpretation of the topic.

Here are some occasions when the preacher may want to choose a topical approach:

- When the subject of the sermon transcends the foci of a single biblical text or theme. A single biblical text seldom contains the fullness of the church's reflections on foundational doctrines or formative practices. A text may provide a point of entry into such a doctrine. A doctrine may help the preacher interpret a particular text. But from time to time, the congregation needs to be exposed to the church's overarching thinking about the doctrine or practice.

- A situation in the congregation or in the wider culture may be so pressing or of such size that the sermon needs to get directly to the work of theological interpretation, and not take the time necessary to offer an exegesis of a biblical text en route. For instance, when a tornado rips through town on Saturday morning, the preacher may need to use the sermon to offer a pastoral theological interpretation of natural disaster in a way that is not contained in any single biblical passage.

- The Bible is silent on many subjects that many contemporary congregations need to consider. As previously noted, the preacher can often get to such subjects by way of analogy or by working from general theological principles assumed by the Bible. This route is often so difficult that the preacher runs out of sermon time before getting to the real issue.

41

- The Bible's perspectives on some themes can be theologically troubling. While the preacher could get to such subjects by preaching against a biblical text or theme, the congregation is sometimes better served when the preacher moves directly to the topic.

- The preacher is often tempted to use a biblical text as a springboard to a topic without taking account of the otherness of the particular biblical text. For example, a text may contain the word *sanctification*. The preacher recognizes that the congregation needs a deeper grasp and experience of the doctrine of sanctification, so the preacher jumps immediately from the text to the doctrine. In the process, the preacher may ignore the distinctive perspective on sanctification in the text and speak as if the text contains the church's full-bodied doctrine.

The topical preacher can make use of biblical texts in the sermon. While the preacher needs to handle such texts in ways that are exegetically appropriate, the sermon is not controlled by the exegesis of the passage in the expository sermon. The preacher turns to biblical texts for the help they can give in interpreting the topic theologically.

A topic can often become the basis for a series of sermons (see appendix C). In this case, a single sermon cannot satisfactorily cover the topic. The preacher divides the topic into subtopics, and considers a different subtopic each week.

The preparation of the topical sermon is similar to the preparation of the expository sermon in that the preacher moves from defining the topic through investigating the background and manifestation of the topic to identifying the salient theological assumptions in the topic. In the next stage of sermon preparation (chapter 3), the preacher will make a normative theological analysis of the topic. I now summarize factors that go into preparing the topical sermon.[7]

(1) How Will the Preacher Define the Topic?

The preacher needs to define carefully the topic that will be the subject of the sermon so that the sermon can discuss the topic in a clear and theologically adequate manner.

For instance, a congregation struggling with its theological identity may ask, *What do we believe?* The beliefs of a congregation seldom derive from a single biblical text, but rather come to expression as the result of reflection on a number of texts as well as theologians from the history of the church. The preacher could preach a single sermon that summarizes the fundamental beliefs of the denomination and the implications of those beliefs. Or, the preacher might create a series of sermons that order the fundamental convictions of the Christian movement of which the congregation is a part.

(2) How Is the Topic Manifest in the Church and World Today, and How Does the Congregation Encounter It and Respond to It?

A key step in the preparation of the sermon is to determine how the topic is manifest in today's church and world. How does the congregation experience the topic? The preacher seeks to describe the congregation's encounter with the topic as fully as possible. The preacher needs to take into account not only ideas that the congregation has about the topic, but also actual experiences that people have with it. These experiences include thoughts and emotions as well as associations of which the Christian community may not be fully conscious.

I suggest that this step come early in the preparation of the sermon because the preacher is not, at this juncture, making a normative judgment about how the congregation *should* view the topic theologically and ethically. The preacher is simply trying to *describe* and *name* the actual relationship of the community and the topic. Of course, a person can never be completely objective and dispassionate when describing something. Elements of interpretation always enter the description. The preacher does not try to put on an objective face, but tries to be conscious of the interpretive factors that innately filter into the descriptive process.

For instance, when preparing to preach a topical sermon on Christian attitudes toward homosexuality, the preacher would want to name how the congregation encounters this topic and the dynamics that are a part of such encounters. *What do we mean by homosexuality? How are homosexual persons portrayed in the news and in the other media that are a part of the congregation's world? Do other*

Christians address members of the congregation on this topic either personally or through the media? Who are the most vocal persons and perspectives that come into the congregation on this issue? Does the congregation include members who are gay or lesbian? Are the latter allowed to describe their own experiences of homosexuality? How do members of the congregation react to these multiple contacts with homosexuality and homosexual persons? What do members of the congregation think? Feel? How does the congregation speak and act *toward homosexual persons when such persons are present?* The preacher will probably identify a spectrum of responses to this phenomenon within the congregation.

A primary resource for this description is the pastor's listening to the congregation. How do they talk about the topic? Image it? React viscerally to it? Along this line, the preacher may actually want to interview some parishioners to let them say for themselves how they experience the topic. The preacher can also note how the topic shows up in everyday settings (for example, at home, at school, in the workplace, at the mall), in the electronic media, in novels, in real-life experiences of the congregation and others. The preacher may also need to engage in research in the library, in magazines, or on the Internet to get a full picture of the topic and the personal and communal dynamics that surround it.

(3) What Are the Origins of the Topic?

Knowledge of the origins of a topic and how the Christian community often helps the preacher and congregation understand that the topic grow out of particular situations and issues. Topics seldom originate as abstract issues, but usually originate with a human face out of deep human questions. A topic is seldom one-dimensional, but usually grows out of a matrix of dimensions, including ideas and questions, feelings (sometimes unspoken), and behaviors. Awareness of the origin not only helps the preacher understand the topic and its importance, but also often furnishes material that the preacher can use directly in the sermon.

The preacher often needs to engage in research. For example, when preaching on the practice of forgiveness in the Christian community, the preacher would want to consult articles in the Bible dictionaries on forgiveness to get a bird's-eye view of forgiveness in the biblical communities. When developing a sermon on a doctrine or practice, or on some ethical questions, dictionaries of church history and theology provide information about the origin of the topic and how the church has understood the topic in different times and through different authors. A good pastoral library should contain such reference works. For discussion of the origins of topics that have not had a prominent place in the history of the church, the preacher may need to go outside the usual theological reference works. The preacher may need to search the local public library or the Internet.

At this point the priesthood of all believers can come into play. Preachers are sometimes called to preach on topics with which they are unfamiliar. Congregations often contain members who are more familiar than the preacher with the origins and manifestations of the topic. The priesthood of all believers goes into action when the pastor consults with such persons. When human and other resources are not available in the church, the preacher may need to seek connections in the wider community. When preaching on an economic question, for example, the preacher may meet with a local college professor who teaches economics. When wrestling with a Christian perspective on the availability of health care in Canada, the preacher might visit a physician who is familiar with health care and its availability and expense.

(4) How Has the Church Interpreted the Topic in the Past?

This question is an extension of the previous one. In fact the preacher can sometimes engage in steps 2, 3, and 4 in a single motion.

Except in the case of topics that have appeared in the world for the first time in the last few years, preachers seldom interpret a topic in a vacuum, but take their places in traditions of interpretation. In this phase of sermon preparation, the preacher identifies how other communities and thinkers have interpreted the topic. The "past" can extend as far back as the world of the Bible (and even farther in the case of topics that have resonance with civilizations older than those in the world of the Bible).[8] The past includes the history of the church. These voices sometimes speak a single interpretation, but sometimes they speak in different accents. The preacher does not have to agree with these voices, but conversations with them often helps the preacher and congregation come to clarity regarding what today's church can believe and do.

For instance, a current topic that could focus a sermon is "family values." The preacher who seeks to develop a sermon on this topic would want to determine the purpose of the family and attitudes toward it in the world of the Bible and in the history of the church. If "the history of the church" seems too big a category, the preacher might look at particular voices within history, for example, Augustine, Aquinas, Luther, and Calvin. The preacher would seek to identify who makes up a family, and the values that are supposed to operate within the family system, and in relationship to the family in the world outside the family. What do people from the past think God wants to happen in family systems? How should a family contribute to the larger world?

To respond to the question of how the church has interpreted the topic in the past, the preacher usually looks up the major voices on the topic in the Bible and in the history of the church, with the help of Bible dictionaries and dictionaries of church history and theology. If the church or individual Christians have not addressed the topic, the preacher may need to go to the library, the Internet, church members, or authorities beyond the church.

The preacher takes into account the teaching of the Christian movement with which the preacher and congregation are affiliated. If the denomination has not adopted an official opinion, the preacher can become acquainted with leading voices from the denominational tradition. In many church circles, congregations today are not bound by statements from the past, but such statements often help the preacher understand why people today think and act as they do.

(5) What Are the Various Interpretations of the Topic in the Church Today?

In preparation for coming to a firm theological interpretation, I find it very helpful to set out the various interpretations of the topic that are alive in the church today. I want to know what others think, and why. I try to hear them as genuine "others." They become dialogue partners as I think about a contemporary interpretation of the topic that will make theological, and other kinds of, sense.

I am often instructed by interpretations in the following categories:

Popular theology is often voiced in the hair-styling shop, on talk radio, and among neighbors up and down the street. Such interpretations are seldom informed by rigorous critical thinking, but I need to know about them because they are often widely shared and deeply held, even if people cannot fully say why.

The *denomination or Christian movement of which the congregation is a part* often has a recent or historic formal statement on the topic. When such a statement is lacking, leading thinkers in the denomination or movement have often thought deeply on the subject. I find such information is not always widely disseminated; so few people in today's congregations are aware that their church or its leaders have thought theologically about the topic.

The *theological family with which the preacher identifies* (for example, evangelical, postliberal, liberation, revisionary) often has clear and even forceful interpretations of the topic.[9] For instance, Wesleyan theologians have a distinctive view of the notion of perfection. Theologians often interpret the topic with differing accents. Indeed, they sometimes disagree with one another, especially on controversial topics.

When the congregation becomes aware of such viewpoints (popular theology, denominational position, major theological schools), the community is often quite engaged. Even when the congregation, or some members, conclude that they cannot support the popular thinking of their friends, or the denomination's public stance, or the riveting statement of a major theologian, the community's interaction with such positions helps the community clarify its thoughts and to recognize the relativities in the thoughts of others.

At this juncture of the preparation of the sermon, the preacher should have a clear sense of the otherness of the biblical text or the topic. However, the preacher needs to be careful not to think that this moment in interpretation has completely finished the identification of the otherness of the text or the topic. Subsequent reflection during sermon preparation may cause the preacher to reconsider conclusions from this early phase.

From the perspective of your exegesis of the text or topic, reflect on your own sermon (or the sermon you heard) that you called to mind after reading the sample sermon. To what degree did your preparation of that sermon honor the otherness of the text or the topic? If you are thinking about a sermon that you heard, describe the degree to which the sermon gave evidence that the preacher honored the otherness of the text or topic? To what degree did you (or the preacher) project your own religious vision, values, or ethics onto the text or topic? Which of the recommended steps in the exegesis of the text or the topic did you include in your preparation? Did you overlook some steps? If you were exegeting the text or topic today, what would you do in the same way? What might you change? If you are thinking about a sermon that you heard, what would you recommend that the preacher do similarly? Differently?

CHAPTER THREE

Is the Sermon
Theologically Adequate?

The purpose of exegesis is to honor the otherness of the text or topic (chapter 2). The next phase in the preparation of the sermon is to name the theological and moral relationship between preacher (and the congregation) and the text or topic. The preacher should not thoughtlessly preach what the text asks us to believe or the popular theology surrounding a topic. The preacher needs to develop a sermon that helps the congregation relate with the text in a way that is appropriate to the gospel, intelligible, and morally plausible.

Most of the time a pastor can preach the gospel through the text or the topic. Sometimes, however, the preacher must help the congregation recognize that the text or the topic contains elements that are not appropriate to the gospel or that are not intelligible. The sermon should then lead the congregation not only to critique the text or the topic from the perspective of the gospel, but also to experience the gospel as good news.

In this chapter, I first offer three criteria by which to theologically analyze texts or topics. The chapter then suggests three possible relationships between text or topic and congregation. This relationship determines the direction of the sermon.

In a sermon feedback session, one of the listeners is assigned to respond to the question, *Was the sermon theologically adequate?* The respondent and the preacher often find it helpful if the respondent gives the feedback in the form of responses to these three questions: *Is the witness of the sermon appropriate to the gospel? Is the*

49

sermon intelligible? Morally plausible? Most of the time the answers to these questions is yes. But sometimes preachers make statements that are inappropriate to the gospel, unintelligible, or morally implausible. Once in a while preachers voice convictions that they do not really believe.

Three Criteria for Theological Analysis

Preachers and students of preaching often say they want to "think theologically" about a text or a topic.[1] Thinking theologically about a text is a process by which the preacher helps the congregation determine what they can—and should—believe from the point of view of the congregation's deepest convictions concerning God, the gospel, and the divine desires for the world. At the same time, thinking theologically includes listening to the text or topic to determine how the text or topic clarifies, amplifies, or deepens the congregation's understanding of God, the gospel, or God's desires for the world. Thinking theologically means coming to a normative conclusion regarding ideas and actions that the church regards as appropriate or inappropriate, intelligible or unintelligible, moral or immoral.

I join Clark M. Williamson, dean of Christian Theological Seminary, in proposing three criteria that facilitate determining a normative perspective on a text or topic: (1) appropriateness to the gospel, (2) intelligibility, and (3) moral plausibility.[2] While these criteria can often be applied straightforwardly, theological interpretation is sometimes complicated and messy. As I noted in connection with exegesis, we never achieve pure and objective theological analysis; thinking theologically is an interpretive process that is influenced by the social and theological location of the preacher and the congregation. We seek to be aware of the biases that enter into theological interpretation.

Recognizing that all theological thinking (and all preaching) contains elements of relativity resulting from our social locations and from human sin, many theologians today speak of coming to relatively adequate theological conclusions.[3] An adequate conclusion results from wrestling with issues of interpretation, recognizing points of relativity, and representing God in ways that are helpful though necessarily incomplete. An adequate conclusion is one that will do for now, though we keep the windows of consciousness open for further insight.

(1) Are the Claims of the Text (or the Manifestation of the Topic) Appropriate to the Gospel?

The preacher reflects on the degree to which it is appropriate for the community to believe what the text or the topic invites the community to believe, as discovered in the exegesis of the text or topic (discussed in the previous chapter). Are the claims of the text or the topic consistent with what the preacher and the congregation most deeply believe concerning God, Jesus Christ, the Holy Spirit, the church, and the world?

To use this criterion, the preacher must have a clear and well-founded understanding of the gospel. In this context, the term *gospel* does not refer to the literary genre of Matthew, Mark, Luke, and John, but takes its cue from the etymology of the Greek term for *gospel*, which means "good news." The gospel is the central message of the Christian community. Preachers should be able to summarize their understandings of the gospel in compact ways so that they can use that summary as norm by which to measure the beliefs of texts and topics.

Our perceptions of the gospel change in response to fresh insight. For a community's understanding of the gospel exists in a dialectical relationship with the Bible, doctrine, and a wider experience in the world. On the one hand, the preacher uses the core meaning of the gospel as a plumb line to measure the witness of a biblical text or topic. On the other hand, a biblical passage or topic text may press the preacher and the congregation to enlarge or refocus some aspect of their understanding of it.

There is no single way of expressing the gospel. Its content can be formulated in many different ways. In fact, Christians sometimes debate how best to understand and speak of the gospel. I follow Clark M. Williamson in thinking that the gospel is the good news that

> God graciously and freely offers the divine love to each and all (oneself included) and that this God who loves all the creatures therefore *commands* that justice be done to them. This dipolar gospel (a) *promises* God's love to each of us as the only adequate ground of our life

51

and (b) *demands* justice from us toward *all* others whom God loves. God's justice and God's love are the two basic modes of expression of the one divine character, God's *hesed* [steadfast covenantal faithfulness].[4]

We come to know this gospel through the life and stories of Israel. It is confirmed for the church through Jesus Christ.

In the Bible and Christian theology, justice is a relational term. The just community is one in which all persons and elements of nature relate with one another in unconditional love. In this community no one is demeaned, deprived, or subjected to violence.

I evaluate all texts and topics through the double lens of God's unconditional love for all, and God's call for justice for all. I ask of each text, and its various elements, *Does this text affirm that God loves each person (and all parts of nature) with unconditional love? Does this text call for justice (that is, relationships of love in community) for each person and all constituents of the natural world?*

When the preacher identifies a biblical passage that is appropriate to the gospel, the task of the sermon is to name and draw out its implications for the contemporary community. This movement may involve clarifying, amplifying, specifying how the text can help the community interpret its present life from the perspective of the gospel, or calling the community to live consistently with the gospel. For instance, Isaiah 40 ("Comfort, O comfort my people, says your God. Speak tenderly to Jerusalem. . . ." vv. 1-2*a*) is such a text. This poem affirms God's love for Israel and God's will to restore the community without impugning or threatening anyone in the community or beyond.

When the preacher encounters an element that is not appropriate to the gospel, the sermon needs to clarify why the text is not appropriate. In other words, the preacher needs to critique the text. For instance, the author of 1 Timothy 1:19-20 says, "By rejecting conscience, certain persons have suffered shipwreck in the faith; among them are Hymenaeus and Alexander, whom I have turned over to Satan, so that they may learn not to blaspheme." It is simply inappropriate for a Christian to place other Christians in the hands of Satan, even if the purpose is to help the delinquent Christians become more faithful. However, as I noted at the beginning of this chapter, the sermon cannot stop with calling attention to the deficiencies of the text, but needs to press ahead to show how the gospel itself offers a more adequate interpretation of the situation. What would be a theologically appropriate manner of helping Hymenaeus, Alexander, and their contemporary equivalents become more faithful disciples?

The assumption in Mark 9:49-50 that God is present and trustworthy in fulfilling the divine promises when the community suffers because of internal or external reasons is certainly appropriate to the gospel. This aspect of the passage affirms God's unconditional love for members of the community and God's desire for the congregation and the larger world to live together in justice. However, the larger apocalyptic theological world of Mark does contain elements that are not appropriate to the gospel. This viewpoint assumes that God is omnipotent—that is, can do all things at any time. The apocalyptic theologians typically assume that all things take place in the world either by God's direct initiation or by God's permission. Apocalyptic theologians think that God either initiates the tribulation or permits it. Either way, God is responsible for directing or allowing intensified suffering. This belief is inconsistent with the notion that God loves the world unconditionally and seeks for its many inhabitants to live in justice.

When the criterion of appropriateness is used in a sermon feedback session, we ask it of the content of the sermon itself. *Is the good news articulated in the sermon appropriate to the gospel?*

Although I have been listening to student sermons for more twenty years, I am still surprised at the number of preachers who say things that they do not truly believe. This phenomenon usually takes place either because preachers simply do not pay attention to contradictions between what they believe and what they say (sloppy thinking), or because preachers use familiar language from the tradition that the preacher has not studied carefully and that does not express what a preacher truly believes. Usually when these things surface in feedback, the preacher is a little embarrassed, but is glad to have the disparity pointed out.

(2) Are the Claims of the Text or the Topic Intelligible?

The criterion of intelligibility deals with our capacity to understand what a text asks us to believe, as well as with our capacity to believe what a text asks us to believe. This criterion is composed of three subcriteria.

(a) *Are the claims of the text or the topic clear enough that we can understand them?* If the preacher has carried out a satisfactory exegesis of the text, we should be able to understand what the text or topic asks us to believe or do. For instance, I have already stated clearly what Mark 9:49-50 invites us to believe.

If the preacher is uncertain about what the text or topic invites listeners to affirm or do, the preacher probably needs to spend some more time in exegesis and reflection. This subcriterion is often provocative in sermon feedback. For feedback, the question is rephrased slightly, *Can the congregation understand the sermon? Are its claims clear enough for the community to grasp them?*

(b) *Are the claims and prescriptions of the text or topic consistent with other things that Christians believe and do?* This subcriterion has to do with logical consistency and contradiction. In order for the preacher and congregation to embrace the beliefs or ethical directives of a text, the content of the text should be consistent with the community's understanding of the gospel. When the various elements of the church's theology are congruent with one another, not only is the Christian community clear about what it does and does not believe and what it should and should not do, but also the community knows what it can and cannot count on from God. The integrity of the church's witness is at stake.

As observed already, the heart of the witness of Mark 9:49-50 is that God is faithful to the community during struggles in its internal life and during struggles with the wider community that result from Christian witness. This idea is consistent with the core convictions of the Christian community. For reasons given in connection with question (c) below, I find it inconsistent with other things that I believe about God and the world to think that the church is living in the last moments of history during an intensification of suffering (tribulation) immediately prior to a single dramatic, apocalyptic moment when Jesus will return. However, I recognize that other Christians find this notion consistent with their understandings of God and history. This difference illustrates the fact of theological pluralism in the Christian house. Christians must decide which interpretations of God and the world make the most sense.

Traffic sometimes runs both ways on the bridge of logical consistency. When the preacher discovers a contradiction between the claims or injunctions of a text or topic and those of the community, the preacher should ask, *Does the logical inconsistency raise a possibility that we should take seriously, even though it would mean reframing some of our thinking and acting?* The inconsistency can invite the community to rethink aspects of its faith.

Once in a while a community may not be sure what it can truly believe about a theological idea or, more likely, a position that the church should take on an issue. In this case, the preacher can explain the situation and can offer some guidance for the interim.

When used in a sermon feedback session, this subcriterion can be adjusted from the text or the topic to the sermon as a whole. *Are the claims and prescriptions of the sermon as consistent with other things that Christians say and do?*

(c) Are the claims and injunctions of the text or topic seriously imaginable?[5] A congregation needs to be able to imagine in a serious way that the claims or injunctions of the text can actually take place. To put it another way, the community needs to be able to believe that what the text promises and commands is true. The church needs to understand how the witness of the text fits into how people understand the world to work today.

This subcriterion is more delicate than the previous ones. As recently as a generation ago, many Christians in North America subscribed to the Enlightenment perspective on the world (sometimes called the modern worldview) that held that things could be regarded as true only when they could be demonstrated scientifically. This view, of course, meant that some Christians had difficulty believing in elements of the Bible, and Christian tradition that appeared to violate natural law.

Hence, preachers needed either to reject many aspects of the Bible and Christian tradition or to find ways of interpreting such elements that did not view them solely in terms of Enlightenment presuppositions. Along the latter lines, preachers would usually interpret the difficult elements by appealing to the difference between surface and deeper meanings, or by taking the difficult elements as figurative language. Many Christians still think along these lines.

However, two things have clouded the Enlightenment view of the world. First, methods of determining truth associated with the Enlightenment and its extensions and refinements in the modern world are not as objective and as reliable as we thought. Many conclusions established by the scientific method have been revised.

For instance, whereas we once thought that Newtonian physics would last forever, Newton's approach has been replaced by quantum physics. Quantum physics may eventually be replaced. Second, whereas the Enlightenment mentality presumes a single worldview, we now know that human communities manifest a pluralism of worldviews. This change is now often referred to as the transition from the modern worldview to postmodernism.[6]

Hence, the preacher and the congregation need to consider what is seriously imaginable from the perspective of the worldview of the community. I operate from a modified modern point of view that moves in the direction of postmodernism by recognizing that it is only one of several possible ways of explaining the world. I affirm things that are seriously imaginable (or that "make sense") within a modified modern worldview.

From my perspective, some of the claims of Mark 9:49-50 are seriously imaginable and some are less so. The idea that God is omnipresent support in times of difficulty is certainly believable. The idea that we are living in the last days awaiting a singular intervention of God is less convincing. Mark wrote almost two thousand years ago and the apocalyptic cataclysm has not occurred, thus calling into question the idea that we are in the last days of the present era of world history. Furthermore, the very idea of an apocalyptic interruption of history is problematic. This way of thinking presupposes a three-story universe with Jesus "coming" from the upper story (heaven) to the middle story (earth). We think of the universe not as a three-story affair, but as infinitely expanding. More troubling is the idea that God has the will and the power to end the suffering of this world but does not do so. If God has the power to end suffering but does not, then God's love and justice are called into question. However, as I point out in the sermon, it is not necessary to think that we are living in the last days to take heart in the deeper witness of the next that God is covenantally faithful.

The worldview of the text may invite the preacher and the congregation to rethink aspects of what they consider "seriously imaginable." I know a number of persons who, as young adults, adopted a secular view of life and who did not think the sacred was seriously imaginable, but who in later years have come to find the sacred an essential constituent of their worldviews.

When used in sermon feedback, this subcriterion (like the previous ones) can be adapted from the text to the sermon as a whole. *Are the claims and prescriptions of the sermon seriously imaginable, that is, can the congregation really expect what the preacher says to be true?*

(3) Are the Claims of the Text or Topic Morally Plausible?

By "moral plausibility," I refer to the moral treatment of all individuals, communities, and elements of nature. A morally plausible text or topic is one that calls for all people and parts of nature to relate with all others in unconditional love and justice. This criterion focuses the norm of appropriateness to the gospel explicitly on social relationships and the social world. If a text or topic calls for, or permits, situations in which persons are denied love or justice, that text or topic is morally implausible and the minister needs to offer a theological and social corrective.

Mark 9:49-50 is a morally plausible text. The passage calls for members of the Christian community to recognize that God is present in love and in desire for justice for them. The passage calls members of the church to "have salt [among] themselves," that is, to live covenantally with one another. This particular text does not deny God's love to anyone, nor does it license injustice in any relationship.

When this criterion is used in sermon feedback, the question focuses not only on the text, but on the sermon as a whole: *Is the witness of the sermon morally plausible? That is, does the sermon assert God's unconditional love for all persons (and elements of nature), and does it call for the communities of the church and the wider world to embody justice for all?*

The foregoing theological analysis usually comes to one of three conclusions. A text or topic may be

- altogether theologically adequate (that is, appropriate to the gospel, intelligible, and morally plausible);

- mostly adequate but partly inadequate (some aspect of the text is inappropriate to the gospel, unintelligible, or morally implausible);

- mostly inadequate (the text is fundamentally inappropriate to the gospel, unintelligible, or morally implausible).

When these relationships are clarified, the preacher is ready to think more specifically about the relationship of the text or topic to the congregation. That is the subject of the next two chapters.

Think about your own sermon (or the sermon that you heard) that you are using as a case study as you read this book. Is the text or topic on which the sermon centers appropriate to the gospel? Is the text or topic intelligible in the sense of being clear? In the sense of being consistent with other things that Christians believe and do? In the sense of being seriously imaginable within your view of how the world operates? Is the text or topic morally plausible?

Transfer those questions from the text or topic to what you, or to what the other preacher, said in the sermon itself. Is the content of the sermon appropriate to the gospel? Is the content of the sermon intelligible in the sense of being clear? In the sense of being consistent with other things that Christians believe and do? In the sense of being seriously imaginable within your view of how the world operates? Is the sermon morally plausible? If the answer to these questions is yes, rejoice. If the answer to these questions is no, how might you (or the preacher) change the sermon in order to make the content appropriate to the gospel? Intelligible? Morally plausible?

CHAPTER FOUR

Does the Sermon Relate the Text or Topic to the Congregation in a Responsible Way?

The purpose of the exegesis of a biblical text or a topic is to identify the otherness of that text or topic. A next phase in the preparation of the sermon is called hermeneutics. The word *hermeneutics* comes from a Greek term that means "to interpret." In preaching, hermeneutics refers to the process whereby the preacher moves from the meaning of a text or topic in the past to the meaning for today's community.[1]

We sometimes distinguish between *exegesis* and *hermeneutics* by saying that exegesis tells what a biblical text *meant*, whereas hermeneutics tells what a text *means*. Hermeneutics is the movement from the meaning *then* to *now*. While hermeneutics is less a mathematically precise science and more an art and an act of the theological imagination, hermeneutics includes some standard perspectives.

In this chapter, I first expand on the possible relationships between the preacher and a text or topic, and the general task of the sermon in regard to each of those relationships. The chapter then turns to the hermeneutical possibilities for the expository sermon (especially the hermeneutic of analogy), and for topical preaching.

The concerns of this chapter are closely related to those of chapter 5, "What Is the Significance of the Sermon for the Congregation?" To determine the hermeneutical relationship of the text or topic with the congregation, the preacher needs a deep pastoral knowledge of the congregation (chapter 5).

In sermon feedback, the title of this chapter puts a helpful focus on the hermeneutical dimension of the sermon: *Does the sermon relate the text or topic to the congregation in a responsible way?* Respondents to the sermon identify the relationship between the text or topic and the congregation by using categories from the discussion below. They reflect on the degree to which that relationship fits the context of the congregation, and suggest ways that the preacher might sharpen that relationship.

Relationships Between the Preacher and the Text or Topic

At the end of the previous chapter, I noted three possible relationships between the preacher and the text or topic. Each of these relationships suggests a different task for the sermon.

(1) When the Text or Topic Is Theologically Adequate

A text or topic is theologically adequate when it asks the congregation to believe and do things that are appropriate to the gospel, intelligible, and morally plausible. Many texts fall into this category. The preacher is called to help the congregation grasp the major claims of the text or topic and identify how those claims relate to the life of the community.

When the congregation is interested in the text or topic and is disposed in a friendly way toward it, the preacher can move directly toward applying it to the life of the congregation. When the congregation is not interested, or resists, the insight of the text or topic, the sermon may need to develop the community's interest, or deal with the resistance.

Psalm 8 is an example of a text that is theologically adequate. This psalm praises God because the divine sovereignty and majesty are demonstrated in creation. It celebrates the fact that the sovereign God cares for human beings and gives them dominion over other elements of creation. The notion of dominion, in this context, refers to exercising power in our immediate worlds in the same way that God exercises power in the cosmic world to bring all things into relationships of mutuality and support.

Psalm 8 is appropriate to the gospel, intelligible, and morally plausible. The preacher needs only to disclose how this psalm alerts the Christian community to God's care for the created world and to help the congregation today understand and put into action this passage's understanding of the nature and purpose of human life (made a little lower than the angels, exercising dominion). The sermon, like the psalm, could explain why and how the congregation would want to praise God for these things.

(2) When the Text Is Mostly Adequate But Partly Inadequate

Many texts or topics fall into this category. In most of these materials, the major theological themes are appropriate to the gospel, but aspects of the texts or topics are unintelligible. The preacher's work is to help the congregation sort through aspects of the material that are theologically adequate, and those that are problematic, and to help the congregation figure out a way to relate them.

Mark 9:49-50 falls into this category. In the sermon, I explain that the core of the text is consistent with our best understanding of God and the gospel, while some of the larger world of the text is problematic, especially at the level of intelligibility. The sermon affirms the adequate dimensions of the text while naming, but not becoming preoccupied with, those dimensions that are not adequate. The unintelligible dimensions are secondary to the overall witness of the text.

In other texts, points of inadequacy are more central to the interpretation of the text and call for greater attention. For example, John 5 tells the story of Jesus healing a person who had lain ill at the pool of Bethzatha (sometimes called Bethesda) for thirty-eight years. This aspect of the text is appropriate to the gospel, for it affirms God's love for the sick person. Jesus healed this person in a single moment, evidently, by means of a single word. This aspect of the text is clear, but it is unintelligible from the standpoint that such things do not normally occur in my world.

This text has a further problem. After the initial healing (vv. 1-9), the text launches into a lengthy diatribe against "the Jews" and shows the superiority of Jesus (and the church) to "the Jews" and to conventional Judaism (vv. 10-45). Most scholars in the long-established denominations today agree that such criticism slips into caricature. It misrepresents the Jewish people of the first century for the purpose of showing that the church superseded Judaism as the rightful heir of the promises of God. This way of thinking (which is found in different degrees in Matthew, Mark, Luke, and John) contributes directly to the rise of anti-Judaism and anti-Semitism. The preacher needs to critique such thinking as inappropriate to the gospel and morally implausible, since it denies that God loves the Jewish people, and as unintelligible, since it fundamentally misrepresents first-century Judaism. The sermon can, further, point the congregation toward ways of understanding the Jewish people and institutions that are more appropriate to the gospel and more just.

(3) When the Text or Topic Is Mostly Inadequate

Relatively few texts or topics fall into this category. Such materials are largely inappropriate to the gospel, unintelligible, or morally implausible. In this case, the preacher's vocation is twofold: to alert the congregation to the theological, intellectual, and/or moral difficulties in the materials, and to bring forward a more adequate understanding of these things.

As an example of this relationship, I have already mentioned the writer of 1 Timothy turning over Hymenaeus and Alexander to Satan. In this case, the preacher would want to help the congregation consider alternatives that are theologically adequate to the objectionable elements. What is a way that is more appropriate to the gospel to help persons whose faith is shipwrecked rather than turn them over to Satan?

Hermeneutics and the Expository Sermon

How does the preacher get from what a text meant to what it means? How does the sermon move from then to now? The *hermeneutic of analogy* is one of the most reliable guides to this movement.[2]

Preachers typically turn to the hermeneutic of analogy when a text or topic is appropriate to the gospel, intelligible (or mostly intelligible), and morally plausible. This hermeneutic is especially useful when a passage is appropriate to the gospel but contains elements that are not directly imaginable in today's world.

The hermeneutic of analogy is based on two ideas. First, the world of the Bible and today's world have many differences. Second, the world of the Bible and today's world share many common experiences that can often be related with one another by means of analogy.

What Is Different in the World of the Bible and Our World?

The world of the Bible and today's world are different in many ways. The physical environment in the Bible lands differs from many physical settings in North America. Not only did they differ from us in dress, houses, modes of transportation, communication, farming methods, and technology, but also in many aspects of their social worlds. For instance, they assumed that slavery was a valid social relationship. Marriages were often arranged at a very early age. Mediterranean antiquity did not have a concept of race as we do; people of color were not victimized by discrimination in the same way as they are today. Religious life also had different qualities. Jewish people in antiquity (and today) had many practices that are not continued by contemporary Christians.

Indeed, without knowing quite a bit about the ancient world, a contemporary person can hardly understand some passages from the Bible. As an example, consider this passage that opens the prophecy of Amos.

> Thus says the LORD:
> For three transgressions of Damascus,
>   and for four, I will not revoke the punishment;
> because they have threshed Gilead
>   with threshing sledges of iron.
> So I will send a fire on the house of Hazael,
>   and it shall devour the strongholds of Ben-hadad.
> I will break the gate bars of Damascus,
>   and cut off the inhabitants from the Valley of Aven,
> and the one who holds the scepter from Beth-eden;
>   and the people of Aram shall go into exile to Kir,
>   says the LORD. (Amos 1:3-5)

To what transgressions does Amos refer? What is the meaning of the peculiar expression, "For three transgressions of Damascus, and for four?" What is Gilead, and who is threshing and why? What are threshing sledges of iron? What are the house of Hazael and the stronghold of Ben-hadad, and why are they burning and being devoured? Why are Damascus, Valley of Aven, Beth-eden, Aram, and Kir mentioned here? Why are the Aramites going into exile? Do I believe that God condemns people and sends them into exile?

With the help of Bible dictionaries and commentaries, I can respond to the above questions. To condense what I find there, God is bringing about judgment on the peoples mentioned above because of various injustices. But, even when this dimension of the message is clarified, I am left with a question: *How does awareness of this oracle and the judgment help a contemporary Christian community?* Differences are easy to identify between the world of Amos and the world of First Christian Church (Disciples of Christ) in Indiana.

What Realities or Experiences in Our World Are Similar to Those in the World of the Text?

The second idea on which the hermeneutic of analogy is based is that people and communities in the ancient and contemporary worlds have much in common. Although many cultural forms differ between the world of the Bible and our world, a common experience often lies below those forms. While people in antiquity and the contemporary world may call things by different names, we have similar thoughts, circumstances, and feelings. Our experience is often analogous to that of Bible times. The preacher seeks to find analogies between the world of the text and the world of people today. A key question is, *What realities or experiences in our world are similar to those in the world of the text?* The preacher can often locate parallel experiences in individual lives, in churches, in communities beyond the church, and in the larger world.

The preacher *looks for analogies in the various elements in the text and the world to which it was addressed.* This is immediately applicable in the case of *documents that directly address a community.* In the case of Amos 1:4-5, the preacher would search for ways communities act unjustly today that are analogous to the injustices perpetrated in the days of Amos. To use the language of the text, *What transgressions in our world are similar to the transgressions of Damascus? Who is threshing a community today in a way parallel to the threshing of Gilead?* Amos saw the downfall of some ancient peoples as divine condemnation because of their violations of covenantal community. What are some ways that groups today are in collapse because of violations of covenantal community?

Stephen Farris, who teaches preaching at Knox College in Canada, finds that it is often instructive to locate an analogy not within the text itself, *but in the community to which the text was addressed.* Farris speaks of these audiences as persons or communities "behind the text."[3] They are not named directly in the passage, although the writer directs the text to them.

For example, Farris turns to the setting for which the book of Deuteronomy was written. Deuteronomy recalls that the Exodus took place about 1200 BCE. However, Deuteronomy was put together during the exile in 597–538 BCE. Farris points out that while the stories tell about events that occurred about 1200 BCE, the writers of Deuteronomy retold the stories with an eye toward encouraging the Jewish community in (or near) exile about 597–538 BCE. The latter community was weary from the events preceding the Exile and from being deported across a lonely desert to new land.[4] They questioned the promises that God had made to their ancestors and to them: *Why did this national tragedy happen? What will God do about it?* Some may have questioned whether the God of Israel was as powerful as the gods of the Babylonians.

This situation suggests parallels between the people to whom Deuteronomy was written and our situation. How are we weary from struggling with the internal life of our community and with its relationship with the larger culture? How can we take seriously the promises of God, given the fact that the situation of the world has not changed very much since the days of Deuteronomy? How are we in exile?

From this perspective, the preacher would show how the authors of Deuteronomy address such questions. The Deuteronomist wanted the community to recognize that as God was faithful to people in the generation of the Exodus, so God would be faithful again to the generation in the Exile. Similarly, God will be faithful to weary congregations today.

Farris's approach underlies the sample sermon on Mark 9:49-50. I reconstructed the historical situation of the community of Mark as one of people living in a time of multiple tensions within the community as well as between the community and the larger world. They called that situation the time of tribulation. Mark used the image of salt to evoke God's covenantal faithfulness during such periods. I do not think that our world is in the throes of the apocalyptic tribulation; however, I still ask, *What are situations of stress and struggle today that are similar to those in the community to which Mark wrote? How do our acts of witness bring down fire? How are our faith and energy sustained for witness when pressed by such difficulty?*

I pause over a vexing hermeneutical issue that is a stumbling block to many preachers: *the portrayal of some Jewish people, theological convictions, practices, and institutions* in the Gospels (and in some other parts of the Second Testament). Jewish leaders, especially the Pharisees, priests, scribes, and Herodians, are often depicted negatively—as rigid, legalistic exponents of works righteousness who repeatedly antagonize Jesus, the disciples, and the early church. As noted before, most scholars today think that this portrayal does not represent historical Pharisees, but is a caricature that the early church has read back into the story of Jesus in order to help justify the separation of the church and the synagogue in the days of the Gospel writers. Preachers frequently employ the hermeneutic of analogy in such a way as to continue, and even magnify, this caricature by asking, *Who in our church (or world) is similar to the Pharisees or other Jewish leaders in a passage?*

For example, when Jesus' sermon at Nazareth in Luke 4 suggests that God's grace is poured out on Gentiles (represented by the widow at Zarephath and Namaan the Syrian), the congregation in the synagogue becomes outraged and tries to throw Jesus over a cliff. The preacher too easily drifts into a harangue on those nasty, rigid, blind, and uncaring Jewish people, and makes an analogy centered in the Jewish stereotype. Who in today's church and world are similar to the rigid, ethnocentric Jewish congregation in the synagogue at Nazareth? This use of the Jewish leaders not only misrepresents the Jewish people of the first century but also reinforces anti-Judaism and anti-Semitism. Hence, this straightforward application of the hermeneutic of analogy is inappropriate to the gospel and is morally implausible.

When dealing with negative portrayals of the Jewish people in a biblical text, I recommend that the preacher explain this presentation and critique it as bad history and bad theology. The preacher can proceed with a chastened version of hermeneutic of analogy by asking, *Who in our world resists the restoring ministry of God through Jesus Christ?* Indeed, the preacher can often locate persons or groups in the congregation or the larger church who frustrate God's renewing work. The sermon can make such moves without casting aspersion on Judaism and its adherents.

A different kind of hermeneutical relationship evolves *when the text is largely inappropriate to the gospel, unintelligible, and morally implausible.* The preacher does need to search for an analogy; but to explain the theological or moral difficulties with the passage and to indicate how the good news of the gospel offer us an alternative understanding of the central motif of the text.

Hermeneutics and the Topical Sermon

Hermeneutics is often simpler for the topical sermon than for the expository one. A topic usually becomes the focus of the sermon because it is of immediate interest to the congregation. The congregation wants to know how to relate to it. A topic often has a history that is important for the congregation to know, but the preacher seldom needs to make an analogy. *The sermon can usually interpret the topic directly.* Indeed, in the sermon itself, the preacher can often employ the criteria of appropriateness to the gospel, intelligibility, and moral plausibility to analyze the topic. The conclusion can be stated straightforwardly.

For example, many congregations struggle with how to understand abortion. Although this topic is quite prominent in the wider culture, I seldom hear a sermon that deals with it comprehensively. Members of the congregation, then, are often left to ponder possible Christian understandings of abortion on the basis of nothing more than propaganda and sound bites from groups along a spectrum of opinion from those that insist that almost all forms of abortion are wrong to those who think that abortion should be freely available.

The preacher could define what is meant by *abortion*; describe how the congregation encounters phenomena related to it; and explore resources from the Bible, the history of the church, and contemporary theology that help the congregation reflect on abortion. The sermon might then name possible interpretations and help the congregation consider those that are relatively more and less adequate.

However, *the hermeneutic of analogy can sometimes provide a model for interpreting a topic.* This approach works especially well with a doctrine or other topic that emerged in a particular historical moment or within a particular set of assumptions in history, but that now seems dated or hard to understand. The preacher could ask, *What circumstances did the doctrine or other topic address? How did the doctrine or topic function in that world? What realities or claims function similarly in our world?*

For instance, the Nicene affirmation of faith (adopted at Constantinople in 381 CE) confesses that the church has four marks: one, holy, catholic, and apostolic. A preacher could develop a topical sermon discussing these four marks, or a series of four sermons in which each sermon focuses on a distinct mark.

At the time of the council, the church was deeply divided on a number of doctrinal issues, such as how to identify a community that was a true expression of the church. The assembly at Constantinople developed the four marks to help the church define its boundaries and to distinguish it from other communities. According to the council, the presence of these marks in a Christian community shows that the community is a true expression of the church; their absence suggests that a community does not manifest the fullness of Christian life.

Consider the mark of the oneness of the church. In the midst of the ecclesiastical confusion in the fourth century, the council intended the mark of the oneness of the church to bring about a uniformity of conviction that made it possible to distinguish Christian from sub-Christian theologies and communities. To be one meant for all Christians in the one true church to affirm the same things. Communities that did not join the uniform affirmation of faith, as interpreted at Constantinople, were not a part of the one, true church. This principle brought about oneness by denying diversity.

Our situation is quite different, but the doctrine of the oneness of the church is still very helpful. The hermeneutic of analogy observes that in the fourth century, the mark of the oneness of the church functioned to help the church recognize Christian identity and relatedness. This hermeneutic asks, *Given the different situation of the church today, how can this mark function similarly for us?*

A key difference between the fourth century and today is that today's churches are increasingly aware of the relativity of all forms of perception and expression. Contemporary Christians recognize that pluralism in doctrine and witness is a given. Our problem is not how to bring about ecclesial uniformity, but rather how to recognize relatedness in a situation of wild ecclesial pluralism. To be sure, the church today still struggles with how far ranging the boundaries of belief and practice can be. The oneness of the church reminds us to recognize and honor commonalities that are essential to community, while respecting differences among communities. In the midst of a fractious world, the doctrine of the oneness of the church allows the Christian community to make a powerful witness by modeling how diverse communities can live together in mutuality and support.

With a grasp of the general relationship between the text or topic and the congregation in hand, the preacher is now ready to think more specifically about how the sermon could apply to the community that will hear the sermon. That is the subject of the next chapter.

Think now about the sermon that you preached (or heard) that is your case study. Which one of the hermeneutical relationships outlined in the first part of this chapter best describes the relationship between the text or topic and the congregation?

If the sermon that you preached or heard was expository, and was largely appropriate to the gospel, intelligible, and morally plausible, did you or the preacher help the congregation recognize points of difference and points of similarity between the world of the text and our world? Did the sermon draw a responsible analogy between the ancient text and the contemporary situation?

If your message or the one you heard focused on a topic that was theologically adequate, did the message help the congregation name this quality, and the reasons for it, and name implications for interacting with the topic today?

If the sermon (whether textual or topical) was inappropriate, unintelligible, or morally implausible, did you or the preacher bring this interpretation into the sermon, and the reasons for it, in a clear way? Did you or the preacher take the next step of articulating an understanding that is more appropriate, intelligible, and morally plausible?

In view of the approach to hermeneutics sketched in this chapter, would you rethink aspects of the hermeneutical movement in your sermon or in the sermon you heard?

CHAPTER FIVE

What Is the Significance of the Sermon for the Congregation?

I have been hearing sermons in class nearly every week since 1982. In addition, I read a lot of sermons and listen to some on audiotape and videotape. Based on this experience, I report that most preachers work hard at exegesis. Most of the sermons are theologically adequate and offer sensible hermeneutical suggestions. However, few preachers relate the major theological concern of the sermon to the congregation and our larger world in concrete ways. Too many sermons remain at a very general level.

For instance, the message might clearly communicate that our identity as a baptized community means that we should love one another. However, the preacher seldom helps the congregation envision how to express love in particular situations in the church and in the community beyond. Who are we to love? How do we love?

This chapter first explores what a preacher needs to know about the congregation and how the preacher can make such discoveries. I recommend that preachers take the time to make an inventory of their own self-awareness. I emphasize the importance of pastoral listening. I stress that the sermon should include at least one life-like story with which listeners can identify. The chapter concludes by suggesting sources for such materials and some principles for using them in sermons.

When asking *What is the significance of the sermon for the congregation?* in a sermon feedback group, we press the respondent to be as specific as possible: "Tell us how the sermon helps you relate the

70

gospel to *particular circumstances* in your personal life, your congregation, and today's world." For reasons given toward the end of this chapter, I also insist that sermons contain at least one lifelike story that brings the good news of the sermon to life. The feedback group discusses the degree to which the lifelike story accomplishes this purpose, and makes suggestions for how the preacher might improve the telling of the story.

Knowing the Congregation

One of the most important pieces of advice given to ministers who begin new pastorates is, "You need to get to know the people." The better the preacher knows the congregation, the better the preacher is able to relate the sermon specifically to the congregation.[1] The preacher wants the congregation to hear the sermon and to name precisely how the gospel message relates to its world. Pastoral listening is key.

A preacher needs information about the congregation on three levels. At a basic informational level, the preacher needs to be aware of what kinds of people are present—men, women, races, and ethnicities, and so forth. At another level, the preacher wants to know the characteristics of the people who make up the listening community as the particular and complex people they are. At still another level, the preacher must be aware that the congregation is more than a collection of individuals. It is a community—a body, a system—that is more than the sum of its individual members. The congregation has a common life with its own personality and characteristics as a group. The preacher does not simply speak to Sue, Fred, Francis, and Pete as individuals, but needs to take into account the corporate identity of the congregation. Sue-Fred-Francis-Pete are a Christian community.

Occasionally in the material that follows, I refer to formal, informal, and tacit levels of awareness.[2] Formal levels refer to things as they are officially authorized or spoken. A constitution and its bylaws, for instance, are the formal authorities of congregational life. A formal mission statement, for instance, may declare that the congregation seeks to welcome new people into fellowship. However, people often talk informally with one another in contexts outside the formal power structures, but in ways that are quite

71

influential in community life. For example, the group of people who meet for a small-group dinner on the second Thursday of the month may not be officially constituted as a decision-making body, but their thoughts and feelings can be very influential in congregational life. This group speaks informally about the fact that they like the congregation just as it is: "We don't want to become a megachurch." Often, the informal understandings within a congregation are more authoritative than the formal. Tacit elements are seldom directly acknowledged, even in informal thought or conversation, but they, too, are often quite forceful. For instance, people simply know that a particular parking spot belongs to Aunt Jane. People in the congregation never, even informally, say to one another, "We will not speak to newcomers," but week after week they give visitors a cold shoulder.

The preacher needs to take into account the full range of factors that make up the life of a community—persons present, relationships, ideas, values, feelings, practices, behaviors, and physical setting and its implications. The pastor wants to have a deep sense of how the people think, feel, and act.

The pastor can pick up some of this data from membership rolls and other easy-to-use sources. But a preacher can get some of this perspective only by disciplined and sensitive listening to the congregation. The preacher needs to discern what they say formally as well as informally, and even tacitly.[3] People sometimes say one thing when something else is really on their minds or hearts. Pastoral counselors refer to this phenomenon as latent content— that is, a message behind the message that a person may be speaking or sending. Furthermore, people sometimes know they are supposed to think, feel, or behave a certain way when they actually think, feel, or behave another way. Attentive listening—especially listening for the latent content and paying attention to the feeling tones of speech, body language, and congruity or incongruity between words and actions—often enables the preacher to listen for the real message that is behind what people say.

To help develop a deep acquaintance with the congregation, I cannot emphasize enough the importance of pastoral calling in the home, workplace, school, and other places that are important to the congregation. Ministers routinely call at times of illness and traumas to render pastoral care. Pastors sometimes make home visits in order to invite people into positions of leadership. However, ministers should also regularly visit parishioners in their homes, workplaces, schools, and recreation sites for the purpose of getting a fuller impression of the community. Seeing people in environments outside of church often reveals much about their values, their hopes, their fears, and their actual commitments.

The preacher can also get a sense of how the congregation feels by paying attention to trends and events taking place in the city, state, nation, and the world. An international incident that galvanizes the attention of the world, persistent national debt, the closing or opening of a manufacturing facility in town, a blockbuster movie, the discovery that the park across the street from the church building is a site for buying and selling drugs—such things affect the ways in which the congregation understands itself and its larger settings.

Each human being is distinct, as is each human community. But human beings share many things in common. Hence, a preacher can often use her or his own humanity as a source of insight into thoughts, questions, hopes, fears, and other phenomena that may be at work in the congregation. If I am anxious about something, I can raise the question of whether members of the congregation might be anxious about something similar.

A preacher wants to get as much of a sense as possible for how the world feels to the congregation. How does a day or a week or a year feel to the listening congregation?

A preacher should also take into account what the congregation expects from the preaching. What does the congregation hope will happen when they encounter a sermon? At times, the preacher may want to shape the sermon to coincide with the expectations of the community. At other times, in order to provoke a particular reaction, the preacher may want to go against the grain of congregational expectation. At still other times, the preacher may want to begin the sermon as if it is going to travel familiar paths, but then take a turn that subverts expectation.

Experienced preachers sometimes counsel younger preachers to imagine that several people from the congregation are in the study during the preparation of the sermon. As the preacher works, he or she carries on an imaginary conversation with the folk in the room. *"Sue, where does the sermon-in-a-sentence intersect with your life?"*

More boldly, John S. McClure, noted professor of preaching at

Louisville Presbyterian Theological Seminary, proposes that the preacher meet weekly with a group of laypeople to talk over the text or topic and possible ideas for the sermon.[4] These people are sometimes called a "feed forward" group, since they feed material forward into the sermon. They raise questions about the text, offer insights and observations, and recount experiences that relate to the developing sermon. These encounters often open windows for the preacher into the heart and soul of the congregation.

Information about who is present, their life orientations, and emotional profile can also help the preacher remember to include materials in sermons over a season of preaching that relate to the circumstances of all the different groups in the congregation.[5] Preachers sometimes unconsciously turn to material that is associated with one group in the congregation, while not including material that relates to others. One woman said, "If I hear another golf story, I will scream."

Questions to Ask About the Congregation

The following questions and categories can help develop a profile of the congregation as a body. In each case, the preacher not only seeks statistical answers to the questions but also needs to name the dynamics at work in the listening congregation. The preacher can take these dynamics into account when preparing and preaching the sermon. For instance, at the statistical level, the preacher asks, *What is the distribution of the congregation according to age (children, youth, the millennial generation, generation 13, the baby boomers, the silent generation, the World War II generation)?* Beyond that, the preacher needs to reflect on the characteristics of each generation in this community. What are their values, hopes, and fears? The preacher further asks, *How do the generations relate with one another? What are points of mutuality? Points of conflict?*

Here are some key questions:

- What is the size of the listening community? The answer to this question includes not only the persons who are formal members, but also nonmembers who attend regularly or who are in the circle of people influenced by the sermon.

- What percentage of the listening community are men? Women?

- What percentages of listeners live in households with two parents and one or more children? How many of these households blend parents and children from previous marriages? Households with one parent and one or more children? Two adults of different genders married to one another? Adults of the same gender in partnership? Single adults?

- What is the makeup of the congregation according to race and ethnicity?

- What is the distribution of the congregation according to age—children, millennial generation, generation 13, boomers, the silent generation, and the World War II generation?

- What are the religious orientations within the community on a spectrum from conservative to liberal?

- What percentage of the congregation are heterosexual, gay and lesbian, as well as persons who are bisexual, transgendered, questioning, and asexual?

- In what kind of setting is the congregation found—urban, suburban, exurban, county seat, small town, rural?

- What is the situation of the congregation's setting with regard to population growth, stability, or decline?

- What are the percentages of the congregation according to social class?

- What is the composition of the congregation by levels of education?

- What cultures are present in the Christian community (for example, southern, Midwest, Far West, Northeast, white-collar, blue-collar, Hispanic, Asian, African American, Anglo American, and so forth), and how do these cultures interact?

- What is the history of the congregation? Which events and relationships from the past continue to shape the congregation?

75

- What values and behaviors does the community most appreciate? From what values and behaviors does the congregation keep its distance?

- What are the most important events and rituals that take place in the life of the congregation on a regular basis (for example, placing a certain kind of flower on the altar table; chicken noodle dinners; mission trips, and so forth)?

- What are the patterns of mental operation in the church? Some people are more deductive and linear in their ways of perceiving the world and thinking. Other people are more inductive and associative.

- How does the congregation understand its mission formally, informally, and tacitly? What are the points of congruity and incongruity among these various understandings of mission?

- What are the physical places that are most important to the congregation (for example, the worship space, or particular things in the worship space; fellowship hall; the walkway to the parking lot)? What is the significance of these places?

- What are the formal structures of power in the congregation? Who occupies those structures? What are the informal and tacit centers of power in the congregation—that is, who is really powerful? How do the formal and informal structures relate?

- Who is on the margins of the congregation? Why are they on the margins? What does their marginality tell the preacher about them and about the community?

- Who speaks up in the congregation, and who is silent?

- What books does the congregation read? What movies or television shows does it watch? To what radio programs does it listen?

Identifying and describing who is present in the listening community should also raise the preacher's awareness as to who is *missing*. Does the ratio of men to women in the congregation reflect the culture at large? What about the ratio of various racial and ethnic groups—Anglo American, African American, Hispanic, Asian, and

Native American? This concern has an important theological dimension. The makeup of the church is supposed to prefigure the great reunion of the whole human family in the realm of God when all peoples are together in mutuality and support. A congregation cannot adequately represent the realm of God when its composition omits persons or groups from the full spectrum of the human community. The preacher may need to help the congregation recognize points at which it needs to enlarge its community to witness to the reconciliation that God intends for all peoples in the divine realm.

Since I was a guest preacher when I preached the sample sermon "Have Salt Among Yourselves," I did not have the advantage of a deep pastoral relationship with the community.[6] I had led a weeknight Bible study in that congregation for several weeks, so I had some familiarity with the congregation and their questions. I talked with the pastor. When I learned that I would be visiting that community, I began to pay attention to items about it in the electronic media and in the newspaper. On Sunday morning, I arrived early enough to drive through town to see what the physical condition of the houses and businesses might suggest about local circumstances. I also walked through the church building to see what it might tell me about the congregation and its values and feelings. Key items that I learned are summarized in the italicized commentary just prior to the sermon itself on p. 13.

Knowing Yourself

Stephen Farris, a Canadian biblical scholar and teacher of preaching, points out that it is important for you, the preacher, to be aware of your own proclivities.[7] In chapter 2, I commented on personal qualities of which you should be aware and on their roles (positively and negatively) in sermon preparation and preaching. To refresh or deepen your self-awareness, you could inventory yourself using the categories just enumerated for getting to know the congregation.

Relate the Sermon Specifically to the Congregation

The preacher wants to relate the sermon as specifically as possible to the congregation and its particular dynamics and setting. As a preacher, I ask, *Given what I know about this community, what are the specific implications of theological and hermeneutical interpretation of the text or topic?*

I find it helpful to think about relating the sermon specifically to the congregation and its world in terms of ever-expanding circles, moving from individuals in the congregation, through the congregation as community to the local setting, the state, the nation, and the world.

- What are the specific implications of my interpretation of the text or topic for the individual lives of persons in the congregation? In a message on divine providence, for example, the preacher can help individuals name particular ways that they experience providence in the home, in the workplace, at school, and in other settings.

- What are the specific implications of my interpretation of the text or topic for the congregation as a community? In a sermon inviting the community to repentance, the preacher could specify some specific things for which the congregation as community needs to repent. For instance, a congregation composed mainly of Anglo Americans may need to repent of the ways it manifests racism. The preacher would need to indicate how the congregation could repent of complicity in racism.

- What are the specific implications of my interpretation of the text or topic for the local setting—the area in which the congregation is located—as well as for the way in which our congregation relates to this setting? For instance, in a sermon on loving our neighbors as ourselves, the preacher might want to help the congregation reflect on the fact that all the people in the area are neighbors. How can the congregation express love for the people who are, literally, neighbors on their block and in their town, including those the congregation usually keeps at arm's length?

- What are the specific implications of my interpretation of the text or topic for the state, the nation, and for how our congregation relates to these settings? A sermon calling for the end of the death penalty, for example, could point out particular

78

ways that the congregation can mobilize opposition to it. How would eliminating the death penalty enhance life in our state?

- What are the specific implications of my interpretation of the text or topic for the global community, as well as for the way in which our congregation relates to these settings? In a message calling for economic justice, the preacher might help the congregation recognize economic injustices among the so-called First World and Third World countries, and identify particular steps the congregation can take to help justice come about in economic affairs among nations. The sermon, for instance, might point the congregation toward specific actions by which it can encourage First World nations to forgive the debts of Third World nations.

A preacher could also think about the possible outcomes of the sermon from the standpoints of different groups in the congregation. What are the implications, for instance, of a biblical text for persons in the congregation who are in the upper economic class? For middle-class persons? For persons in poverty? For the relationships of persons in the different classes with one another in the context of the covenantal community?

In the sample sermon on Mark 9:49-50, I found a primary point of contact between the text and the community in the experience of moving from a feeling of joy and confidence in witness to one of discouragement. Many of today's listeners were once enthusiastic and confident in witness, but are now troubled and even disheartened.

I asked, *Given what I know about this community, what are the specific implications of the exegesis of the biblical text and its theological and hermeneutical interpretation? In what specific situations do members of this community experience discouragement that is similar to the discouragement faced by the Markan church? In what ways do today's people need to experience the renewal of the divine promises?*

In the last third of the sermon, I named several circumstances that I knew—through previous contact with the congregation and through talking with the pastor—were a part of their world in which they follow the path from initial positive expectation to discouragement. I mention the difficulties that accompany watching a child mature into a surly youth, the ache that accompanies the

79

transition of a relationship from the joy of marriage to the day that one of the partners must live in a nursing home, and the uncertainty that came with the move of a congregation from unanimity around a controversial issue to conflict. These three situations do not exhaust the circumstances of discouragement in the congregation. I hope the listeners will use them as examples from which to identify other similar situations.

In the story of the visit of the chaplain from South Africa to the institute where I was teaching in Zambia, I seek to show how the divine promises to the Markan community can also encourage the county-seat congregation today. This process comes with some disclaimers. For one, a preacher can seldom discuss all of these implications in a single sermon. To treat responsibly all of the possible levels of implication in one sermon would make the ordinary message far too long. A preacher must decide which outcomes are most important to the particular congregation on the particular Sunday that the sermon is preached.

Most of the time the preacher will want to bring out the implications of the sermon for the community as clearly as possible. However, from time to time, the preacher may not want to state the significance of the sermon directly, but may want to put the congregation in a position to sort out the implications for themselves. In this case, the sermon needs to leave the congregation with enough data and perspective to be able to continue thinking and feeling the main themes of the sermon.

Including a Lifelike Story That Brings the Good News to Life

One of the most effective ways a preacher can help relate the sermon specifically to the life of the congregation is to tell at least one lifelike story that brings the good news of the sermon to life. A lifelike story captures the tensions of the text or topic and the complexities of life in the listening community. Indeed, I make it a rule that nearly every sermon should contain at least one such story.

The older literature of preaching often admonished preachers to make sure that the sermon contained illustrations—stories that illustrate the main ideas of the sermon. This way of thinking intimates that conceptual thought is the primary mode of human knowledge. Indeed, one of my teachers said, "An illustration is a substitute for thought."

In recent years, however, many preachers recognize that human knowledge is a gestalt in which thought and feeling are interwoven.[8] I can express some things that I know in concepts and ideas, but I know some things intuitively. I may not be able to articulate fully in conventional language (or even in poetry or other artistic modes of expression) something that I know, but it is still a part of the way I understand the world. A story is not a substitute for thought, but is a different form of knowledge.

A story does not simply illustrate an idea, but creates an imaginative world into which the congregation enters, and which adds to the knowledge of the congregation at the levels of feeling and intuition as well as through ideas. The story should express the main gospel message of the sermon and show the implications of God's unconditional love and universal will for justice in action. Such a story shows how the main claims of the sermon relate to the world of the congregation. It gives the congregation a visual picture.

When listening to the story, the congregation has an imaginative experience of the events in the narrative. When we hear the story, through our imaginations we enter the setting, identify with the characters, and follow the plot. What happens in the story happens to us. It activates our thoughts. It stirs our feelings. It prompts us to envision how we might act. The story adds to the reservoir of experience out of which we live.

I emphasize the importance of the story having the character of good news. Frankly, a preacher can more easily find stories of sin, pain, injustice, death, and other aspects of brokenness than stories of forgiveness, restoration, justice, and love. A story is usually a point at which the sermon has the most profound impact on the congregation. Indeed, telling a story of human pain often brings the congregation to profound silence as they feel the pain of the story. However, if stories in sermons represent only sin and its consequences, the congregation may eventually—perhaps unaware—conclude that the power of sin and brokenness is greater than that of God, love, and justice.

To be sure, a sermon needs to name and describe sin, injustice, and death. But even more, the preacher needs a story that brings the good news to life. A story of good news verifies the claim of the sermon that God is present and active for the good of the world. It also gives the community a sense of power from which the people can live on the basis of the good news. It alerts them to be aware of—and responsive to—God's regenerative purposes in other moments of life. It generates a sense of power for witness.

Toward the end of the sample sermon on Mark 9:49-50, I tell a story from our family's summer at a school in Zambia. This story recollects the situation of the participants from South Africa and a visit to them by a chaplain whose hand had been blown away when he opened a package that contained a bomb. A racist had sent him the bomb to protest the chaplain's witness for justice in that land. The situation of the chaplain and the South African students is similar to that of the church to which Mark wrote. I think that members of the congregation in which I preached this sermon could identify with these circumstances.

The story shows how the main claim of the sermon is true, namely that God is faithful even when our witness to the divine love and will for justice brings us into conflict with others. I hope that the description of the joy of the South African reunion will stir the congregation's awareness of the divine presence with them and will empower them to witness. I try to tell the story in such a way that the listeners are not only cognitively aware of the events that took place in Zambia, but that they experience the intermingled senses of joy, power, and determination for witness in that gathering.

Ordinarily a preacher should save the most powerful story for the later stages of the sermon. By that time, the preacher has created a kind of sermonic nest within which to lay the story so that the story can bring the sermon to a significant moment of insight, recognition, awareness, or climax. By listening to the story, the congregation experiences a world that is shaped by the gospel. The listeners leave the sermon empowered to continue to live out of that world.

Preachers sometimes want to begin the sermon with a story to help generate congregational interest in the sermon. While this arrangement sometimes accomplishes its purpose, it can also work against the sermon. If the preacher has only one good story that embodies the good news of the sermon, then the high moment of the sermon often ends when the sermon is only a few minutes old. The rest of the sermon is, relatively, less engaging. If the preacher follows this pattern week after week, some people become accustomed to listening for the first few minutes of the sermon, but then changing to other channels.

If the preacher begins the sermon with a story that speaks of the brokenness of the world, the sermon needs to contain another story of equal or greater emotive power that represents the good news of the gospel. If a good news story is not present, the congregation may feel that the bad news is more believable than the good.

When beginning the sermon with a story, the preacher needs to be sure that the narrative does not engage the congregation so powerfully that they are unable to leave the world of the story and follow the rest of the sermon. I have heard some stories at the beginnings of sermons that have overwhelmed me so much that all I could do was ponder the story.

Sources of Lifelike Stories

Where does a preacher get lifelike stories? The answer is contained in the question—in life itself. Your everyday experience is a continuous source not only of stories but also of questions, issues, hypotheses, feelings, and insights that can become a part of a sermon. Conversations in the classroom or with colleagues in the lounge often become stories that can illumine sermons. Sitting in the waiting room at the doctor's office or standing in the checkout line at the supermarket may become a moment of revelation.

In the sermon, a preacher may recount an event that actually took place. He or she could narrate a novel, a short story, a play, a movie, or a television comedy that has the qualities of actual experience. Newscasts and interview programs on radio and television often bring forward stories that can help give flesh to the sermon.

When borrowing a story (or other element of the sermon), the preacher needs to acknowledge that the story is not his or hers. Integrity and humility require as much. When the source would be meaningful to the congregation, the preacher can cite it directly: "I heard a story on National Public Radio this week that won't leave me alone. . . ." If the source is not well known, citing it in full might distract the listeners. Instead, one could say something like, "I read a significant thinker in the church this week who says. . . ."

Some messages come alive when the preacher makes direct

reference to people and situations in the listening community. The preacher might recount an event involving Fred, Sue, Francis, and Pete. However, the preacher must first secure permission from the persons involved. Otherwise, they may be embarrassed or feel violated.

Preachers can also make up stories. I was shocked the first time I heard Fred Craddock make this suggestion. But the Bible contains stories that are obviously made up. For instance, the prophet Nathan created the story of the rich person who stole the impoverished neighbor's beloved lamb to feed a guest (2 Samuel 12:1-15). Jesus composed parables. The Danish theologian Sören Kierkegaard fashioned parables. Of course, when creating one's own story, one needs to signal the congregation that it is not a report of an actual occurrence, but is an imaginative construction.

One of the hot debates among scholars of preaching in the last fifteen years centers on whether preachers should tell stories from their own lives and name them as such. On the one hand, some preachers think that preachers should seldom refer to themselves directly. They claim that when preachers narrate experiences from their own lives, the congregation stops thinking about the content of the story and begins to focus on the character and person of the preacher.[9] For example, a pastor may tell a story about being in pain. According to this line of thought, instead of focusing on the idea that the story is intended to communicate, the congregation worries about the well-being of the preacher. If the preacher wants to draw on a personal experience, the preacher should rewrite it in the third person. Instead of speaking in the first person—about "my pain"—the preacher could describe someone in a similar kind of pain.

On the other hand, many preachers think that the preacher can make direct use of autobiographical material to help bring the sermon to life.[10] Preachers can use their own life stories to help the congregation imaginatively experience sin and grace, judgment and redemption. Preachers should tell such stories not to call attention to themselves, but to help the congregation interpret their world from the perspective of the gospel. Of course some personal material does not belong in the pulpit.

While I recognize that ministers can abuse stories from their own lives in preaching, I lean toward the second view. In the sample sermon, I use a personal experience in the last story. I was present for the events. However, the focus of the story is not on me but is on something that I witnessed.

When working on a sermon, how does a preacher remember stories and other material for the sermon? I find that the very act of preparing a sermon sparks ideas and calls forth memories and associations. The anticipation of the sermon prompts me to recognize and remember experiences, books, plays, journals, movies, and other resources.

Furthermore, many preachers find it helpful to keep a notebook or computer file of materials that sound like they might be promising for a sermon someday. For instance, a preacher might jot down a lyric from a song.

I encourage preachers to avoid using stories from collections of sermon illustrations. Almost every time I hear such a story, it fails to resonate with real life. It sounds stale. Many tales from collections are just too simple or too contrived. Often the wording is artificial. While I was preparing this book, a friend said, "When I hear a canned illustration, I just tune out." As a listener, I am moved by stories that bubble up from the world of the preacher and the congregation.

Think now about the sermon you preached, or heard, that you are keeping beside you as you work your way through this book. What are the specific ways it relates to the congregation in which you preached or heard it? As a part of this reflection, consider how many of the "Questions to Ask" above you could answer for the congregation for which you developed, or in which you heard, that sermon. In view of the discussion in this chapter, if you were developing that sermon again, are there things you now think you should know that you did not have in mind when you prepared the sermon? If so, how would you go about discovering them? And how might they affect your sermon? Could you (or the preacher you heard) more directly draw out the particular implications of the sermon for the listening community?

Review the sermon that you preached or heard for stories. Does it contain at least one story? Are the stories lifelike? Does at least one of them embody the good news that is the heart of the sermon? Are they placed in the sermon for optimum effect?

CHAPTER SIX

Does the Sermon Move in a Way That Is Easy to Follow?

In previous chapters, I discussed basic things needed to develop a sermon. You now need to put together the sermon itself. In this chapter, I first note that a preacher needs to decide whether to select a movement for the sermon from stock patterns or whether to create a movement. I describe and illustrate the two basic patterns by which sermons move—deductive or inductive—and consider ways of beginning and ending.

To repeat a mantra from earlier chapters, sermon preparation does not always follow in steps that go "one, two, three." Early in preparation, you may sense a possible movement for the message. Even when that happens, it is good to pause and reflect critically on the degree to which your initial hunch is optimum for this sermon.

In sermon feedback, I pose this issue: "Were you, the listeners, able to follow this sermon easily?" I ask the group to describe their experience of listening to the sermon: *What happened in your mind and heart as the sermon unfolded?* Follow-up questions are often, *If you were able to follow the sermon easily, what helped you? If not, what got in the way, and what might the preacher do differently if preaching this sermon again?* The group focuses on the beginning and ending. *Did the sermon begin in a way that invited you to want to listen? Did the sermon end in a way that encouraged you to continue responding to the sermon with thoughts, feelings, or actions?* Along the way, I encourage the group to name qualities of the sermon that helped the congregation *want* to pay close attention, and qualities that did not encourage them to do so.

Select or Create a Movement

A preacher can put together the sermon itself by selecting a movement from a stock of established patterns, by creating a movement for the particular sermon in preparation, or by adapting a stock pattern. The preacher considers the approach to preaching that he or she prefers, the congregation, and the purpose of the sermon.[1]

I identify some stock patterns below. While a preacher may begin with a stock pattern, he or she often adapts that approach. Many preachers create a fresh approach to the sermon each week. The preacher's process of preparation generates questions, exegetical material, ideas, stories, quotes from theologians, and other material. The preacher arranges how these things unfold in the sermon. One of my colleagues identifies each of the chunks of material for the sermon on three-by-five-inch note cards, and arranges and rearranges them on a blank desktop until a promising flow emerges.

Two advantages of using a preexisting sermon form are efficiency and clarity of purpose. The preacher does not become frustrated or waste time trying to figure out *how* to say *what* he or she wants to say. However, stock genres can be wooden. They may not fit the person the preacher is, or the people to whom he or she preaches, or the purpose of his or her sermon.

An advantage of developing one's own approach is that he or she can shape the sermon to accommodate the congregation and occasion. Another advantage is that it allows for creativity. A potential limitation is that the preacher can become frustrated, and burn up a lot of time, when the creative process is blocked. Also, some preachers have difficulty arranging material in a way that allows the congregation to follow it easily.

A volume that I edited, *Patterns of Preaching: A Sermon Sampler*, includes thirty-four different approaches to preaching (with example sermons), ranging from stock models to movements that preachers create. This list of types mixes forms (genres), purposes, and other matters, but illustrates the wide range of possibilities: [2]

- Puritan plain style (beginning, exegesis, application, ending)
- Sermon as journey to celebration

- Sermons that make points
- Preaching verse by verse
- Thesis-antithesis-synthesis
- From problem to assurance
- Bipolar preaching
- Sermon as theological quadrilateral
- Simple inductive preaching
- Form of text shapes form of sermon
- Four pages
- Sermon as plot and moves
- From oops to yeah
- From first naïveté through critical reflection second naïveté
- Movement of images
- Drawing from the arts
- Sermon develops as author develops novel
- Portrayal of biblical character
- Jigsaw puzzle
- Wedding homily
- Funeral homily
- Topical preaching
- Tracing biblical theme
- Doctrinal sermon
- Sermon on Christian practice
- Teaching sermon
- Preaching on personal issue
- Preaching on social issue
- Group study
- Preaching from perspective of evangelical theology
- Preaching from perspective of liberation theology
- Preaching from perspective of postliberal theology
- Preaching from perspective of revisionary theology
- Preaching in postmodern perspective

After reading *Patterns of Preaching*, a pastor wrote, "I never knew there were so many different ways to preach." However, these possibilities are only a small number out of a much larger range of possibilities from past and present.

Two Basic Patterns of Movement

A preacher typically uses one of two basic patterns of movement in a sermon: deductive or inductive. Preachers use these terms to refer to the broad movement of a sermon. A preacher sometimes puts together a sermon that combines these two approaches.

Deductive Movement

In deductive sermons, the preacher states forthrightly the major claim of the sermon near the beginning of the message. It is as if the preacher puts up a billboard at the front of the worship space saying, "Here is the point of today's sermon." The congregation thus knows the subject of the sermon (and, often, what the preacher thinks about it) from the opening moments of the sermon.

The great virtue of deductive preaching is clarity. However, this approach does have some potential drawbacks. When the congregation knows the direction of the sermon and its major claim, the sermon loses the element of curiosity, even suspense, that often motivates people to follow a sermon. Furthermore, deductive forms are not always adequate to full-bodied experience in the world. Life, learning, and discovery are often less deductive than inductive. If the preacher announces an idea the congregation finds offensive, many listeners will not follow the sermon but will tune out, turn off, and may even seethe.

STATE THE MAJOR CLAIM OR SUBJECT AT THE BEGINNING

One of the first tasks in the deductive sermon is to help the congregation get the major claim or the subject. For an example, I began a deductive a sermon on Ephesians 2:1-10 this way:

> Suppose you're having coffee with a friend at the mall after worship. Your friend is a serious and thoughtful person, a moral person, but not a churchgoer. Your companion puts down the coffee cup, gives you a serious look, and comments, "I know you go to church every Sunday. But I've never known quite why it is so important to you. So I wonder if you would tell me. What is the most important thing in Christianity to you? What keeps you going week after week?" *(Slight pause).*

89

Well, what would you say? What is the most important aspect of Christian faith to you?

The writer of Ephesians gives us a clear answer to this question in the passage that we just read: justification by grace through faith. This pithy summary, of course, prompts other questions. What *is* justification by grace through faith? What does it mean?

I want to unpack these notions with you now: justification, grace, and faith. And I want to explain why many Christians think that they are the central reality of Christian life.

The preacher thus summarizes the major claim of the sermon and indicates how the sermon will develop: a series of discussions that fill out the ideas of justification, grace, faith, and their intertwining.

A variation on the deductive beginning is for the preacher not to state the full claim of the sermon, but to give the subject of the sermon. The preacher indicates the direction of the sermon and what it is about without revealing the content of the message. When preaching deductively, I tend to use this approach because it both orients the congregation to the direction of the sermon while also creating a little bit of curiosity. I began a sermon for the First Sunday of Advent on Luke 21:25-36 (a text that describes the apocalyptic return of Jesus from heaven) as follows.[3]

> When I think of Advent, I think of the smell of greenery, the shimmering of the candles, the Advent hymns. I look forward to the Christmas pageant, the carols, and the mystery of the midnight Christmas Eve service.
>
> So, the scripture lesson we just read is a little bit of cold water. We hear not about Joseph and Mary treading toward Bethlehem, nor three visitors from the East carrying their gold, frankincense and myrrh, nor the shepherds joining the oxen beside the crib. No, we hear about distress among the stars, the moon, and the sun, and fear and foreboding among people.
>
> Why do we begin Advent with this stark text about the return of Jesus on a cloud with power and glory as redeemer of the world and judge of the living and the dead?
>
> Many preachers today would approach this text by means of imagination, story, and poetry. I can certainly imagine a sermon on this text along those lines. But sometimes we need to speak plain thoughts. What do we really believe about the Second Coming? In the spirit of honest and straightforward conversation, I want now to highlight four ways this passage helps us as we begin Advent.

The sermon then sets out four ideas (mentioned below) that specify how the text helps the congregation make sense of the world.

Arranging the Body of the Deductive Sermon

After indicating the direction of the sermon, the preacher develops the major claim or the subject matter of the sermon so as to show how the main concern of the sermon relates specifically to the congregation. The development of the body of the message can take place in a number of different ways. I now briefly mention several. These examples are just that—examples. The preacher needs to choose or create a movement that will serve this part of the sermon.

Preachers often associate deductive preaching with making "points."[4] While deductive sermons sometimes contain points, they need not necessarily do so, as indicated in several of the methods for developing deductive sermons below. Preaching that makes points can be an effective witness to the gospel. However, this style should not be a straitjacket into which the preacher binds every sermon; it does not fit every preacher, every listener, every congregation, every occasion, or every biblical text or topic. One needs to be able to preach in other modes for listeners who are not such linear thinkers, for occasions that are more prone to feeling and impression than to logical analysis, and for texts, doctrines, practices, and other topics that are diminished when they are explained in points. When preaching in this genre, the points must relate directly to the subject of the sermon, to one another, and to the congregation.

I return to my message on Luke 21:25-36 to illustrate deductive development of points. After the beginning (described above), the sermon develops as follows: First, the passage reminds us that the work of redeeming the world, signaled by the birth of Jesus, is not finished. The birth is only an early chapter in the restoration of the world. Second, the passage helps us recognize that the restoration of the world is not simply a touch-up, but a fundamental regeneration. God aims to create a new earth.

Third, the passage helps us think about what we truly believe about the Second Coming. I do not anticipate a singular moment

91

when Jesus will return in an apocalyptic cataclysm that interrupts history. This first-century language points to the fact that God will not stop working to bless the world until all things are as God intends. While I do not anticipate an apocalyptic event, I live with hope because I believe that God is always ahead of us, trying to lure the creation toward a future of love and justice in all relationships.

Fourth, the passage warns us against becoming preoccupied with the timing of the completion of redemption. The text encourages us to spend our time witnessing to God's regenerative activity and not speculating about the end of this world. The passage guides us toward a way of living that helps us participate in God's restoration of the world. These points state several major implications of the passage for the congregation.

A preacher can sometimes *derive lessons or insights from a biblical text or theological doctrine.* The preacher uses major ideas from the biblical text or doctrine as the major divisions of the development of the sermon. Thomas G. Long, one of the best-known preachers in North America today, cites an example from a sermon on Psalm 19:1-14.[5] This passage identifies three ways that God communicates with us. The preacher articulates three main points from these three major motifs.

- God speaks through nature (Psalm 19:1-6).

- God speaks through the divine word (Psalm 19:7-11).

- God speaks through our life experiences (Psalm 19:12-14).

In the case of each medium (nature, word, experience), the preacher needs to explain how God speaks, and how we are able to distinguish divine communication from other things that happen in that medium.

The body of the sermon may *offer reasons the claim of the sermon is true.* In this instance, the preacher asserts the major claim of the sermon and then explains why the congregation can believe it. In a message on "Why We Can Believe in God Today," I assert that it is reasonable to believe in God in our postmodern world, and then review the classic arguments for the existence of God.[6]

Reason 1: The existence of the world implies the existence of a First Cause.

Reason 2: The complex design of the world implies a designing Deity.

Reason 3: The presence of moral intuition implies a source for this intuition.

Reason 4: The fact that we can think of God implies the existence of the One about whom we think.

The sermon notes that no single argument can carry the whole freight for thinking that God exists. But, taken together, these reasons imply that belief in God is reasonable. We cannot prove that God exists, but we can conclude that belief is not irrational.

Another familiar movement is *historical development*. The preacher could trace how the church's understanding of a text or topic has developed over time. The preacher could start with the Bible, identify voices in the history of the church, contemporary perspectives, and offer a clear delineation of the preacher's own viewpoint.

A minister can develop some subjects in connection with the *various groups to whom the subject is related*. For example, after stating the big claim of the sermon, the preacher might explore its relationship to individual persons, the congregation as community, the village (town or city), the nation, and the world.

Needless to say, the number of categories by which the preacher could enumerate deductions of the main point is almost limitless.

WHEN DO YOU PREACH DEDUCTIVELY?

When would you turn to a deductive sermon? This approach is suited to dealing with questions that are consciously in the minds and hearts of the community. The preacher correlates the questions with the sermon. Deductive preaching also lends itself to texts, topics, and circumstances that require quite a bit of information in the sermon, and about which pastor and people can think in a logical, and linear manner. I find that deductive preaching is especially useful in communities with a lot of persons who are new to Christian faith and who need basic orientation. Deductive sermons are excellent vehicles for preaching Christian doctrine and denominational beliefs. Most of the time, a minister would avoid deductive preaching when the sermon deals with a controversial matter. As already indicated, if the pastor begins the sermon by advocating a controversial thesis, the congregation may become hostile and cease to listen.

This approach to sermons particularly fits preachers who are linear thinkers. Preachers who are intuitive and who are gifted in poetry, metaphor, and story will likely be more inclined toward inductive preaching. However, nearly every congregation occasionally benefits from a deductive sermon.

Inductive Movement

In inductive preaching, the preacher does not state the major conclusion of the sermon until near the end.[7] The preacher begins with particular questions, data, and other information, and leads the congregation through a process of consideration that arrives at a conclusion. Whereas a model for deductive preaching is holding up an oral billboard in the pulpit, a model for inductive preaching is taking a journey on which neither the route nor the destination is fully known. The congregation has a general sense of the subject matter of the sermon, but they do not know the precise conclusion until near the end of the sermon.

One of the strengths of inductive preaching is that its process of moving from question or issue to conclusion reflects the way we usually operate in life. We usually move from particulars in experience (incidents, issues, information) to generalizations. The inductive sermon creates a lifelike sense of encounter, reflection, and resolution.

Another virtue of inductive preaching is that it creates a sense of curiosity in the congregation. This quality encourages the congregation to continue listening to the sermon until they hear how the sermon comes out. Still, another strength is that the congregation joins the preacher in the process of reflecting on the text or topic. By so doing, they often have a significant sense of ownership in the conclusion, for they share in the process of discovery that leads to that conclusion.

Inductive preaching calls for considerable creativity from the preacher. Not only must the preacher determine what to say, but also the preacher must determine how to say it. There is no formula, outline, or movement for the inductive sermon.

94

However, this approach has some potential drawbacks. Candidly, I must say that some inductive sermons are almost impossible to follow. They never quite start, go anywhere, or arrive. The preacher appears to say whatever comes to mind, without relating it to what precedes or follows. While stream of consciousness may be high art in a James Joyce novel, it is usually an experience of frustration for a congregation. The inductive preacher needs to be certain that the sermon starts somewhere, moves in a way that the congregation can follow, and goes somewhere.

The process of creating the inductive sermon is sometimes time-consuming and frustrating. The deductive preacher has a general structure into which to pour thought, whereas the inductive preacher is sometimes uncertain how to get from one question or perspective to another to a conclusion, and can even experience the equivalent of "writer's block."

Some listeners prefer deductive preaching to inductive. This orientation is not a matter of intelligence, but of pattern of mental operation. Some people are simply wired, so to speak, as linear thinkers. Other people are wired to move more naturally inductively.

HOW DOES THE INDUCTIVE SERMON UNFOLD?

The inductive sermon begins by calling attention to a question, an issue, an event, a feeling, an experience, or some other aspect of life that calls for interpretation from the perspective of the gospel. This subject may arise from a biblical text or from life experience. The preacher may start by talking about issues raised by the Bible or doctrine, and then move to theological reflection. Or, the sermon may start with issues or incidents from a life outside the Bible or doctrine, and thence go to theological reflection. The body of the sermon brings together the resources necessary to interpret the text or topic.

At some point, usually in the last third of the sermon, the inductive preacher states the major point of the sermon. Sometimes the preacher even articulates the sermon in a sentence. I say "usually in the last third of the sermon" to indicate that the preacher has considerable freedom as to when to make the major point. Sometimes the preacher saves the major conclusion until the last sentences of the sermon. At other times, the preacher recognizes that the major conclusion needs some elaboration, and so makes it earlier. The preacher then fills out implications of the big point. Occasionally an inductive preacher does not state the major claim of the sermon; the preacher leaves the listeners to figure out the primary message of the sermon.

The sample sermon "Have Salt Among Yourselves" (Luke 9:49-50) begins with observations that create a low level of tension. What does it mean to be "salted with fire"? In the early part of the sermon, I do not indicate the specific subject matter of the sermon, much less the major claim. I count on the congregation following the sermon because they are curious about what to make of the interplay of fire and salt.

The sermon then explains the two major images of fire and salt. The explanation of salt has its own inductive character as I review various ways of understanding salt, but come last to the one that is pertinent to this sermon: salt bespeaks covenant. The message mentions that people in antiquity remembered the covenant when they ate food flavored with salt. I hope that people who hear this sermon will also remember the covenant when they experience a salty taste.

I take a similar approach to the motif of fire, beginning with happy associations, then moving to tribulation. I hope that the language describing the fire burning on the inside and the outside of the Markan church is vivid enough for the congregation to feel the heat. The tension of the sermon is at its tightest, for the congregation, when raising the question of how to taste the salt when we experience the transition from a promising beginning to a difficult and even painful development (as baby to teenager, wedding to nursing home, support to rejection).

The major conclusion comes about three-fourths of the way through the sermon. How can the listeners make their way with faithful witness through tribulation? By having salt among themselves. "Remember the promises of God. Remember that God is always with you . . . especially in the fire."

The story of the chaplain's visit to the students in Zambia creates an imaginative experience of the major conclusion. I hope that the listeners feel not only the fire of tribulation, but also the regeneration and energy for witness that come from remembering the promise.

EXAMPLES OF INDUCTIVE MOVEMENT

Although I have rightly noted that the inductive preacher creates the movement of the sermon afresh each week, it still may be helpful for beginning preachers to consider some models for inductive sermons. I offer four sample models. Only the number of preachers limits the number of possibilities for the movement of inductive sermons.

Fred Craddock, one of the most well-known preachers at the beginning of the twenty-first century, suggests that the *process of preparing the sermon can be the structure of the sermon itself.*[8] The preacher re-creates in the pulpit the process of encountering the text or topic, and identifying the questions and issues that it raises for the preacher and the congregation. The sermon traces how the preacher researches the background materials necessary to understand it, and reflects on the theological interpretation of the text or topic.

The preacher sometimes takes the congregation down dead-end paths, or may invite the congregation to sit in the silent contemplation that sometimes gathers around an aspect of text or topic. The preacher may share a quote from a systematic theologian, or a poem or short story, or an experience that comes to mind. Of course the preacher cannot recall every twist and turn that took place during the preparation process, but must focus on key elements that help the congregation follow the path that leads to the conclusion of the sermon.

An inductive message often develops along the lines of *an author developing a novel.* An author begins with general ideas about the purposes of the novel, its setting, the characters, the plot, key events, and the impression that the novelist would like for the book to leave on the reader. The book often unfolds according to plan. However, in the process of writing, the plot and characters may take on a life of their own. The plot takes turns and twists that the writer did not anticipate. The characters say things and act in ways that the author did not have in mind when beginning to write. The novel may turn out to be very different from the one the writer planned.

Similarly, a preacher sometimes sits down with a text, exegetical information, theological insights, and intuition about the relationship of the text to the congregation. As the preacher works, the

97

sermon takes on a life of its own. Ideas and connections appear in surprising ways. The sermon may turn out to be different from the one the preacher expected.

An inductive sermon can sometimes be compared to *taking a journey.*[9] A trip begins at a certain place, and ends at a certain place. Along the way, one stops for fuel, food. Unexpected things happen, too. Beautiful vistas that are not marked on the map suddenly come into view. A roadside stand may be irresistible. Construction can cause delays and detours. One may get a speeding ticket or run out of gas. An accident turns one's world upside down. The person arrives at the destination sometimes exhilarated, sometimes shaken, sometimes perplexed, sometimes relieved, and sometimes prepared to leave on another trip right away.

A sermon, similarly begins with a text or topic, and proceeds toward an interpretation of the significance of that text or topic for the community. Along the way, the preacher picks up fuel and food in the form of information from the commentaries, Bible dictionaries, and other helps. The preacher may come upon facts or insights that are arresting in their beauty, or in the questions they raise. Human experience may function like an accident on a trip, bringing the conventional forward theological movement of the sermon to a halt and even rendering it dysfunctional. The preacher may need to carry out a salvage operation in order to finish the sermon.

An inductive sermon may also be compared to *putting together a jigsaw puzzle.*[10] When starting with a jigsaw puzzle, the pieces are scattered across the table. The process of assembling the puzzle is one of considering each piece and testing how it relates to other pieces. Initially, progress may be very slow as one tries to piece together a border, or some other part of the picture, around which to assemble the pieces. Periodically, the person's eye catches a trait that suggests that several pieces may fit one another, even though they belong to a part of the picture that is not the person's central focus right now. Piece by piece, the picture begins to emerge. As more pieces are in place, the person finds that it is easier to get other pieces in place, and the process becomes faster and faster until the last piece is popped in.

In a comparable fashion, the preacher puts an inductive sermon together by considering various pieces from the Bible, Bible commentaries, church history, systematic theology, current events, as well as experiences from the community and his or her own life. The preacher identifies these pieces, and helps the congregation figure out how they fit with one another, and how they form a big picture.

When Do You Preach Inductively?

When would you turn to an inductive sermon? Such a sermon is good for almost any Sunday. Inductive preaching can bring the congregation into an encounter with the gospel in connection with most biblical texts or topics.

This style of preaching is especially amenable to texts and topics about which the congregation has questions. Inductive preaching is also a good way to approach texts and topics that have an aesthetic dimension, or around which emotions are intense. It allows the preacher an optimum opportunity for poetic expression, the use of imagery and narratives. Because the inductive pattern itself is close to life experience, the preacher can easily incorporate discussion of feelings that are deep and sensitive.

As previously noted, this approach is especially useful when the sermon moves into a controversial direction. Instead of throwing the major claim of the message in the face of the congregation, as is done in the deductive sermon, the preacher eases the congregation into the subject in a spirit of mutual exploration of why the issue is important, how various people are affected by the issue (and feel about it), how different Christians have interpreted the issue (and why), and how the congregation might relate to the issue today. The sermon is less a confrontation and more a journey of exploration and discovery.

However, inductive preaching can take on sameness from week to week that is anesthetizing and even wearying. Congregations can feel a sinking in their hearts at the thought of taking a trip every Sunday, just as they can get tired of deductive preaching that, week after week, parades points through the pulpit. Some inductive preachers have a penchant for developing surprise endings. But how often can a congregation be surprised? Inductive preachers need to monitor their sermons to be sure that they provide enough variety to nurture congregational interest.

Beginning and Ending the Sermon

A good beginning welcomes the congregation into the sermon, while an awkward beginning can actively discourage the community from listening. A good ending can help the congregation take the sermon into their minds, hearts, and wills, while an awkward ending can leave the congregation dangling.

How Can I Begin the Sermon?

The purpose of the beginning of the sermon is to invite the congregation into the sermon. We used to refer to this part as the introduction, but that is not quite satisfactory. Few sermons actually introduce a text or a topic to the congregation. A sermon usually picks up on a question, issue, text, or event that is already alive in the congregation or in the wider world. The early part of the sermon thus does not so much introduce the congregation to the subject, but begins the next phase of the community's consideration of the issue. The beginning phase alerts the congregation to the subject of the message and brings them on board.

There is no one formula for beginning a sermon. Here are some possibilities:

- Point out a peculiarity, an irony, or a theological difficulty raised by the biblical text or the topic.
- Tell a story from personal experience.
- Pick up on something in the life of the congregation or the denomination.
- Connect with an event from the wider world.
- Ask a question.
- Recall or create a circumstance that raises an issue.
- Draw from a movie, a television program, a novel, a short story, or a poem.
- Quote from a figure from church history or a contemporary theologian.

- Refer to a day of the Church Year (for example, First Sunday in Advent, One Great Hour of Sharing Sunday, and so forth).

- Give a lively preview of the content of the sermon.

While a preacher can begin many different ways, a key is for the beginning of the sermon to have an inviting tone, while pointing to the direction of the sermon.

In the following, René Rodgers Jensen, co-minister of First Christian Church (Disciples of Christ) in Omaha, Nebraska, moves deftly to indicate that the sermon will deal with the realm of God. The pastors invited the congregation to suggest topics for preaching and discussed them in a series entitled "You Asked for It."

> Jesus talked about it more than anything else in his ministry. Every week we pray for it to come. Yet most of us, if push came to shove, would have a hard time saying exactly what the kingdom of God (or the realm of God) is. So I was both pleased and somewhat intimidated when one of the requests for our "You Asked for It" Sermon Series was on the realm of God. For while no concept was more central to Christ's own preaching, and so to our own faith, few concepts are more elusive and more difficult to pin down.[11]

The beginning connects the content of the sermon directly to congregational interest and suggests its importance for Christian faith and life. The subsequent sermon explains the theological content of the realm of God and its significance for the community.

Rebecca Button Prichard, a systematic theologian and minister of Tustin Presbyterian Church in Tustin, California, begins a sermon on Pentecost with a personal experience.

> Twice I've lived overseas; and even though they speak English in Australia and Scotland, in both cases I had to learn to communicate. On my first day as a young teacher in a country town in Australia, a student came to my desk and asked, "Miss Prichard, could oi 'ave a lend of your biro?" I stared at him blankly, and then guessed what he meant when he picked up my Bic pen and looked at me expectantly. I quickly learned that a pullover sweater is called a jumper, and a jumper is called a pinafore, and a sweater with buttons is called a cardigan. Lunch is dinner and dinner is supper, and supper is a late-night meal. I came to realize that a car has a bonnet, not a hood, and a boot, not a trunk. I also learned to decipher the Aussie twang.

101

When my folks came to visit, they were lost. My dad called for room service in the hotel. I watched him grow frustrated and heard him firmly [say], "Nine? We're not on nine. We're on fourteen." I took the phone from him and found the lady asking, "Your nime, please?" She needed his name, not his floor. Later, on a tour of Canberra, the capitol, we visited the department of "commas." My dad asked the guide, "What's that?" "Tride," said the guide. Dad drew a blank. I translated, "Commerce, trade."

Communication isn't always easy, and there are times when we need a translator, an interpreter, a go-between. Divine/human communication isn't always easy, either, but the Holy Spirit is the great communicator, the one who helps us understand God's word, and who helps God understand us, and who helps us speak God's word, and to sing God's praise.[12]

The sermon then leads the congregation into reflecting on how the Spirit helps us understand the divine word, helps God understand us, helps us witness to the divine word, and to praise God in song.

Barbara Brown Taylor, a sensitive preacher from the Episcopal Church, developed a sermon on Matthew 10:34-42, in which a part of the mission of the Matthean Jesus is to set father against son, mother against daughter. The beginning picks up a troubling aspect of the text. The preacher has just finished reading the passage.

This burr from Matthew's Gospel is one of those passages I wish he had never written down. I wish a gust of wind had scattered all his notes and blown that page away. I wish he had forgotten all about it until he was done with his Gospel and there was no place left to put it. I do not like this passage, because it seems so contrary to what we need in the world right now. The [North] American family is so fragile, so fractured. The last thing we need is another reason to be set against each other, especially a reason decreed by Jesus himself. The last thing we need is a Lord who strides into our living rooms with a sword in his hand to chop us apart. Most of us are already so chopped apart that he would be hard-pressed to put any more distance between us than is already there.[13]

In the context of naming many forms of pain that beset contemporary families, the sermon explores how our true identity as children of God allows us to live in gospel witness in our family and other relationships.

In connection with the importance of including at least one life-like story in the sermon (pp. 80-85), I have cautioned against beginning the sermon with a story that is emotionally overpowering. The congregation may be so overwhelmed that they cannot continue to follow the sermon.

Preachers sometimes begin the time designated for the sermon with a joke or other remark that does not relate to the message. After telling the joke, they launch the sermon. Preachers take this route to loosen up the congregation and/or to create a bond with the community. However, this technique works against the purposes of the sermon. It confuses the congregation by intimating that the subject of the joke or other remark is also the subject of the sermon. When the joke is finished, the congregation must adjust its expectation of the sermon. Sometimes I get so frustrated by trying to figure out the change in direction that I check out of the sermon and into planning the lecture that I must give in class on Monday night. Sometimes I even feel betrayed when the joke suggests a sermon about an important matter, or at least an interesting one, but the sermon turns to something insignificant or dull. Here is a rule: do not make a remark at the beginning of the time designated for the sermon unless it helps welcome the congregation into the sermon itself.

How Can I End the Sermon?

The purpose of the ending of the sermon is to encourage the congregation to continue responding to the sermon in the moments, hours, and days that follow. We used to refer to this part of the sermon as the conclusion, but that is not quite satisfactory. The word *conclusion* suggests that the process of dealing with the sermon has ended. While the sermon proper must end, the preacher typically hopes that the processes of thinking, feeling, and willing sparked by the sermon will continue.

Again, there is no single formula for ending a sermon. Possibilities for ending are similar to the possibilities for beginning.

- Indicate how your perspective has changed on the peculiarity, an irony, or a theological difficulty raised by the biblical text or the topic.

- Tell a story from personal experience.

- Comment on how the main drift of the sermon applies to the life of the congregation or the denomination.

- Suggest how the sermon affects your view on events in the wider world.

- Ask a question that you hope will linger with the community.

- Recall or create a circumstance that shows how the community can live in the future, given the insights of the sermon.

- Draw from a movie, a television program, a novel, a short story, or a poem.

- Quote from a figure from church history or from a contemporary theologian.

- Reinforce the significance of the sermon for the day of the Christian Year.

- Give a lively and artful summary of the sermon.

The key is for the ending to prolong the effects of the sermon in the heart, mind, and will of the congregation.

Prichard ends a sermon on the significance of the Lord's Supper by recalling her experience as a pastor at St. Giles Church, a well-known Presbyterian congregation in Scotland:

> In St. Giles, where I served as a minister, we had communion [the Lord's Supper] every week. The people would form a circle around the communion table and pass the loaf and the cup to one another. We would drink from large silver cups hundreds of years old. The communion table is at the center of the cathedral, under the tower. The ceiling high above the table was painted dark blue with golden stars, like the sky. Each week as I would lift the cup to drink, I would see the reflection of those stars in the wine—a sign for me that heaven and earth were one in that moment.
>
> At this table heaven and earth come together. At this table we pray for the coming reign of God's shalom, on earth as it is in heaven. In this meal, this Christ-centered, Word-inspired family meal, we gain the power and the sustenance for our life, as God's own in this world. And at this table, there is always room for one more, for it is a table of welcome and hospitality.[14]

When the congregation receives the bread and the cup, they, too, should feel a oneness between heaven and earth, at least for a moment, and hospitable toward others.

Barbara Brown Taylor shows that the ending of the sermon can artfully, even evocatively, summarize the major point.

> That is what love is, Paul says: not a warm feeling between like-minded friends but plain old imitation of Christ, who took all the meanness of the world and ran it through the filter of his own body, repaying evil with good, blame with pardon, death with life. Call it divine reverse psychology. It worked once and it can work again, whenever God can find someone else willing to give it a try.[15]

As the preacher leaves the pulpit, I find myself thinking of situations in which I can express love in the manner of Christ.

Marjorie Hewitt Suchocki, a teacher at Claremont School of Theology, begins a sermon on Hebrews 12:18-24 with a play on the distance between the name of Los Angeles ("city of angels") and the repressive circumstances found in many quarters of that city. She explains that God seeks for the cities of this world to become ever more like the city of God (as discussed in the Bible, the writings of Augustine, and other Christian visionaries). She emphasizes that the congregation can be in partnership with God in re-creating our cities in the image of the city of God, and ends with these questions.

> You are people with the future ahead of you. Will you live in these earthly cities of ours as ones who dare to bring the righteousness of God with you? Will you dare to let that stream of righteousness that makes glad the City of God flow through you? Will you as citizens of God's city be a blessing of justice to this earthly city? The future is before you: God's future is before you. And you have the opportunity so to open your lives to God's justice that through you God will yet bring justice, righteousness, peace to the earthly city. And when you dare to choose to do this, then God's own hope hovers over our cities. They may yet indeed be touched by an angel, redeemed by a cross.[16]

As this sermon ends, I feel the force of these questions. I ponder them. *Am I ready to live day to day with righteousness?*

I venture into semi-sacred territory with this last suggestion.

105

Many preachers end their sermons by saying "amen." By so doing, they intend to indicate that God speaks through the sermon (to which the people say "amen"), and that the act of preaching is also an act of prayer. However, for many Anglo American congregations, the speaking of "amen" in that moment is a signal that they can stop thinking about the sermon and can start thinking about something else. The preacher's "amen" thus often works against the purpose of the ending of the sermon. I recommend that preachers typically avoid ending the sermon with the word.

Whether prone to deductive or inductive preaching, a preacher needs to recognize and strengthen his or her gifts and inclinations. At the same time, he or she needs to develop the capacity to preach in other modes.

Remember the sermon that you preached or heard and are using as a case study. Could the congregation follow it easily? What qualities of the sermon helped the congregation keep track with you or with the preacher? Perhaps you can identify qualities that frustrated the congregation from following the sermon. Could you (or the preacher) make some changes in the sermon to help the congregation follow it?

Was the sermon more inductive or deductive? What were the clues? Comment on how the pattern of movement—inductive or deductive— added to, or frustrated, your experience of the sermon.

Think about the beginning and the ending. What was inviting about the beginning? To what degree did the ending encourage the congregation to continue responding to the message? What, if anything, might you (or the preacher) do differently to help the beginning be more welcoming, or the ending to prompt deeper reflection?

At this stage of your development as a preacher, would you think of yourself as a more deductive or a more inductive preacher? It would be good to name some specific steps you can take both to enhance your capacities as an inductive or deductive preacher and to broaden your range so that you can preach effectively in both modes.

CHAPTER SEVEN

Does the Preacher Embody the Sermon in an Engaging Way?

A sermon does not truly become a sermon until the preacher steps into the pulpit and speaks it in the presence of the congregation. The ways in which the preacher and congregation engage one another in that moment contributes significantly to the congregation's response to the sermon. *How can your voice and body in the act of preaching help the congregation enter the world of the sermon?*

A generation ago, the subject of this chapter would have been called "delivery." However, that designation sounds as though preachers have the same relationship to the sermon as letter carriers have to the mail that they deliver. Today, we speak of this aspect of preaching as "embodiment," for the whole self of the preacher brings the sermon to life, and the listeners receive the sermon in their whole selves—minds, hearts, and wills.

In this chapter I first mention the importance of spirituality, presence, and tone in embodiment. I then discuss several basic categories of embodiment, such as the voice, eye contact, and gestures. Finally, I turn to whether to use a manuscript, notes, or nothing at all in the pulpit.

As noted earlier, if you want to hear an audio recording of the sample sermon on Mark 9:49-50, you can find it on the Internet (www.cts.edu/bookstore/sermons.htm). Below I discuss how I intended to embody that sermon. You might reflect on the degree to which the sermon embodied what I hoped.

When a feedback group turns to this question, we ask, *Did the preacher embody the sermon in an engaging way?* The members of the group are asked to identify qualities in the embodiment that both encouraged them to listen attentively to the sermon and discouraged the community from doing so. We specifically explore whether the tone of the embodiment fit with that of the content of the sermon, the degree to which the preacher was truly herself or himself, and whether the preacher seemed fully present to the community. Along the way, we review how well the preacher could be heard (and otherwise used the voice), as well as the eye contact, gestures, use of the manuscript or notes, and other movements.

Spirituality, Presence, and Tone

The embodiment of the sermon should be characterized by spirituality, presence with the congregation, and tone. These qualities are hard to describe, but when they are present, the congregation usually feels a strong bond with the preacher. When they are absent, the congregation usually senses that something is missing.

By *spirituality*, I mean the sense that the preacher has a deep and genuine spiritual life and that the sermon is born out of the preacher's struggle to understand the text or the topic in relationship with God. The spectrum of honest spirituality runs from robust confidence and trust in God through intimate knowledge to profound doubt and agonizing questions. The preacher cannot just inject a little spirituality into the sermon or cannot consult a checklist of "marks of spirituality" and include them in the sermon. Spirituality emanates from the core of the preacher's being.

By *presence*, I mean the sense that the preacher is truly present to the congregation. The preacher needs to signal that he or she is attentive to the congregation and is emotionally, intellectually, and physically open to the community. Unfortunately, I frequently hear sermons in which preachers appear to be self-absorbed or self-impressed. They may not focus on the congregation in the moment of preaching, but be distracted by other things. The preacher can be standing in the midst of the congregation talking but not be truly *with* the community. Again, there is no inventory of characteristics to determine presence, but the congregation draws more deeply into the sermon when they sense it.

The preacher's way of speaking and acting in the pulpit needs to be consistent with the ways the preacher relates with the congregation in other aspects of life. Preachers sometimes speak in a "pulpit voice" or move in peculiar ways that differ dramatically from the ways that they speak and move at other times. Such differences communicate that preaching is a contrived moment and not real life. The congregation becomes suspicious that the preacher is not genuine but, as one listener said, "puts on an act." To be sure, the preacher in the pulpit often needs to speak more fully to be heard, and make bigger gestures than when having a conversation in the study or teaching a Bible class, but the preacher's voice pattern and demeanor need to be consistent with the way the preacher is in other moments.

The tone of the embodiment of the sermon should be consistent with its theological content. When the tone of embodiment differs from the tone of the content, the integrity of the sermon is undercut. The preacher who tells the congregation, "Be joyful!" in an angry tone of voice leaves the congregation confused. When the message speaks of the joy of knowing God, the messenger should speak in a joyful way. When the sermon deals with sadness, the preacher should speak in a sad tone. When the text or the topic leads the congregation to struggle with God, the sermon needs to have the feel of a struggle.

To get a trustworthy report on how the congregation perceived the spirituality, presence, and tone of the sample sermon on fire and salt in Mark 9:49-50, I would have to interview members of the listening community. Since such interviews did not take place, I can only report my perception of the congregation's response. I tried to wrestle with a question directly concerning the relationship of God with struggle and suffering in witness. I had a palpable awareness that the congregation was involved in the sermon, especially in the last third when the sanctuary became more quiet than usual. I could see that many in the congregation were following the sermon closely. The audiotape confirms that the overall tone of the embodiment was positive but sober, which is consistent with the tone of theological content.

Voice, Eyes, Gestures, and Movement

The voice, eyes, hands, and movement are not simply mechanical aspects of the moment of preaching but are part and parcel of *embodiment*. The preacher can work on them, but in so doing he or she is not simply improving techniques, but is helping the sermon come to life.

The preacher needs to speak in a full enough *voice* that the congregation can hear the sermon easily. When the congregation has difficulty hearing, they often lose attention quickly. Furthermore, one needs to speak with variety in his or her voice (loud, soft, fast, slow) to help the congregation maintain an interest in the sermon. If one's voice pattern is always the same—even if it is loud—it has a narcotic effect on the listeners. The preacher may want to have someone in the congregation signal him or her if the volume becomes so low that the congregation has difficulty hearing.

Furthermore, preachers want to inflect their voice so that the vocal tone matches what they are saying. When asking a question, for instance, their voice should sound like a question. A surprising insight should have the quality of surprise. Most preachers find that practicing with an audiotape in advance of the sermon, and listening to an audio or videotape after the sermon enhance their use of the voice and other aspects of preaching.

When people make *eye contact* with one another, they usually feel that a significant human contact takes place. Eye contact usually helps the congregation feel that the preacher is present with them. Much of the time, when people do not make real eye contact, the other persons do not quite trust the interaction that has taken place. I say "usually" and "much of the time" because there are sensitive moments in life when direct eye contact works against heart to heart communication. A preacher may want to avoid eye contact when it makes the congregation feel too exposed, too vulnerable, or otherwise so self-conscious that they cannot continue listening to the sermon. Once in a while, a particular thought in a sermon may not be suited to direct eye contact. For example, when speaking pensively, a preacher might naturally look, for a moment, out the window or down at the floor.

The preacher needs to know the sermon well enough to be able to look at the congregation quite a bit during the event of preaching. Preachers should look directly into the eyes of the listeners, and not at the wall just above their heads. When the preacher habitually looks at the wall, the congregation may think he or she does not want to relate with them or that the preacher fears them. Listeners often find it dull when a preacher's eyes are glued to the notes or manuscript.

Preachers should *move their hands, arms, and the rest of their body,* in ways that enhance the content of the sermon and that are consistent with their personality. While there may be occasional moments when, for emphasis, the preacher wants to assume a rigid persona, the preacher who is typically immovable in the pulpit is usually boring.

Again, gestures and other movements need to fit the content of the sermon. A clinched fist in a sermon on peace may cause the congregation to think that the preacher speaks one way about peace but acts another (clinched fist = violence). A gentle sermon should contain gentle movements. A sermon whose content is energetic and exciting calls for gestures and other actions that are energetic and exciting.

I find that this aspect of delivery is often particularly difficult for students. Most students think that they are much more lively in the pulpit than they are. Watching a videotape of one of their own sermons often helps them identify things on which they need to work.

Student preachers are often very self-conscious about gesturing and otherwise bringing life to the sermon. In the early stages of preaching, they often find it helpful to force themselves to gesture, even when they do not feel like it, and even when the gestures develop awkwardly. When they continue to do so over several weeks, they begin to gesture more frequently, less self-consciously, and more naturally.

One of the most effective things the preacher can do is to *pause* in the sermon at key moments. A pause calls attention to what the preacher has just said. It allows the congregation to ponder or otherwise process the preacher's remarks. It can create a holy moment in which, in the silence, the preacher and congregation feel deeply present to each another and to God.

In the early moments of preaching the sample sermon, I wanted to have quite a lot of eye contact with the congregation so that we could have the sense of real engagement with one another. I tried to keep the tone inquisitive, but not heavy. Because people often think the Bible is dull, I attempted to communicate that the biblical backgrounds of Mark 9:49-50 are interesting and important by keeping my rate of speech brisk, by maintaining consistent eye contact, and by gesturing quite a bit (for example, I made a little gesture that depicted Elisha throwing salt into the polluted spring outside Jericho). Nonetheless, I could feel the attention of the

111

congregation lag a couple of times during this part of the sermon. I needed to be more energetic.

I wanted to emphasize the important line, "I am your God. You are my people . . . and I will continue to work in the world until it comes." I knew these ideas would recur as leading motifs in the rest of the sermon, particularly at the very end. For emphasis, I tried to speak slowly, deliberately, and with intensity and full eye contact.

After describing the way the tribulation was viewed in the world of Mark, I paused briefly and changed tones of voice before saying, "I imagine few of us think about the tribulation this way." I wanted the embodiment to bring forth a little tension to signal the struggle that I have with the theology of the text. In the next part of the sermon, "The church to which Mark wrote . . . ," I wanted the congregation to feel the fire burning in both the ancient and contemporary communities. To underline the contemporary feeling of fire, I paused before and after "Sometimes life is a fire . . . And sometimes it turns faith and witness to ashes." After that bracing comment, the tone lightened when describing the promising moments of life (birth, marriage, cheering), but then tightened again when the fire "returns" with the teenager, nursing home, and rejection.

The next paragraph summarizes the meaning of the sermon: " 'Salt is good,' Mark says . . . Remember that God is always with you . . . Especially in the fire." I try to speak this section slowly, deliberately and with eye contact that looks into the souls of the congregation. A pause at the end of that section is supposed to give a little time for the meaning to settle into the listeners' hearts.

The embodiment is less intense at the beginning of the story of the visit of the chaplain from South Africa, but as I tell about the chaplain losing his right hand, my own feeling of anguish comes out. When the story makes the transition from anguish to hope, I try to capture the quality of hope born out of suffering in my voice. I pause around several significant lines.

Just before the end of the sermon, I do something that I very rarely do: sing a line from a hymn. Actually, I don't quite sing but kind of chant the line in a way that, I hope, recollects singing. A huge pause follows. The manuscript of the sermon contains another short paragraph. However, in the moment of preaching, I had the intuition not to speak that paragraph. The line from the hymn seemed to create a moment that needed no further commentary. So, I stood at the pulpit in silence for a few seconds, and then slowly made my way to my seat while the pastor moved to the front of the church to offer the invitation to discipleship.

Preaching with or Without Notes?

Students always want to know whether to preach with a manuscript, with notes, or with nothing at all. I can only answer, "You need to find the approach that most helps you in the moment of preaching."

A manuscript allows you precision of wording, awareness of how long the sermon will be, and a wonderful sense of security that you know what you will say. If you take a full manuscript with you into the pulpit, you need to have the content of the manuscript in your heart so that you do not keep your eyes buried on the printed pages, but use the manuscript only for prompting. You can also be so attached to your manuscript that you refuse to make changes that might help the sermon take account of events since you finished the manuscript.

The use of notes gives you the direction and security of a manuscript while taking less time to prepare. You may also feel a little freer to make changes to the sermon while you are preaching, in view of the people who are present or things that happened on Sunday morning. However, when using notes, you may not manifest precision of expression. Also, some preachers who use notes have a tendency to expand the length of the sermon.

The great virtues of preaching without using a manuscript or notes can be immediacy of presence with the congregation, spontaneity, and a natural quality of embodiment.[1] I say "can be" because preaching without manuscript or notes is not magical by itself. Preachers in this mode can be as flat as the most dull manuscript reader. Among the potential dangers of preaching without notes are losing your place in the sermon, and of letting your spontaneous thoughts increase the length of the sermon to the point that the congregation finds it tedious. Some preachers retain the security of having a manuscript or notes by keeping a manuscript or notes under the pulpit or tucked in a Bible while preaching.

You need to find the approach to the use (or nonuse) of manuscript or notes that allows you an optimum feeling of confidence and relating with the congregation while you are preaching. To reach that awareness, you may need to experiment with different modes of preaching.

I preached the sample sermon from a full manuscript. I had marked key words and sentences on the manuscript with different colors of highlighter and with notes made by a pen to both prompt my memory of the content and to remind me how I wanted to try to embody various sections of the sermon. A couple of times my eyes stayed more focused on the manuscript than I wish they had, or than they needed.

Think one more time about the sermon you gave, or the sermon you heard. Does that sermon reflect honest spirituality? If so, how was that sense of spirituality communicated? Did you feel present to the congregation, or did the preacher you heard seem present to the congregation? Did the congregation seem to respond as if the preacher were present to them? If so, what were the clues? If not, what might you, or the preacher, have done differently to be more present? Was the tone of the embodiment consistent with the content of the sermon?

Review the use of the voice, the eye contact, the gestures, pauses, and other aspects of embodiment in the message that you gave or heard. To what degree did each of these things help the congregation feel positively involved in the sermon, or leave the congregation feeling distant from the sermon, or even frustrated by it? Take a moment to identify things you can do to help reinforce or improve the use of the voice, eye contact, gestures, pauses, and other movements.

Do you prefer to preach with a manuscript, with notes, or with nothing in front of you? Reflect on why you have this preference. Perhaps you can preach in other modes to see how they feel to you.

Most ministers find it useful to watch themselves preach on videotape from time to time. You can then assess your embodiment and note things to reinforce as well as things on which to work.

APPENDIX A

Sequence of Steps to Prepare a Sermon

This appendix brings together steps in sermon preparation discussed earlier in the book and summarized in narrative form on pp. 23-25. This list does not account for every wrinkle of the preparation of every sermon, but is a general guide. When preparing a sermon, the steps may take place in different sequences; some steps may disappear, and others may be added. In parentheses, I give page numbers where the step is discussed in the book.

1. Be sure that the sermon arises from your real spiritual life and struggles (pp. 118-19). Pray to be sensitive to the Spirit in the process of preparing the sermon.

2. Review what you know about the congregation—joys, values, questions, hopes, struggles, and fears (pp. 70-77).

3. Select a text or topic as the focal point of the sermon, taking account of the context of the congregation, the season of the Christian Year, and other factors (pp. 29-30, 120-24).

4. Carry out an exegesis that identifies and respects the otherness of the text or topic (pp. 30-48).

   a. For *exegesis of a biblical text*, the following questions are good launching pads:

      (1) What are the natural starting and ending points of the text (p. 33)?

(2) What is the historical setting of the passage, and what is the purpose of that passage in that context (pp. 33-34)?

(3) What are the meanings of the key words in the passage (pp. 35-36)?

(4) How does the literary context help us understand the passage—both the larger setting and its immediate setting (pp. 36-37)?

(5) What is the literary style and function of the passage (pp. 37-39)?

(6) What does the passage invite its listeners to believe—about God and the divine purposes? About the world? About the human response to the divine presence (pp. 39-40)?

b. For *exegesis of a topic,* the following questions are good beginning points:

(1) How do you define the topic (pp. 42-43).

(2) How is the topic manifest in the church and world today, and how does the congregation encounter and respond to it (pp. 43-44)?

(3) What are the origins of the topic (pp. 44-45)?

(4) How has the church interpreted the topic in the past (pp. 45-46)?

(5) What are the various interpretations of the topic in the church today (pp. 46-47)?

(6) What interpretation do you find most credible?

5. Reflect theologically on the witness of the text or topic.

a. Are the claims of the text or topic appropriate to the gospel (pp. 51-53)?

b. Is the witness of the text intelligible—understandable, consistent with other things Christians believe, seriously imaginable (pp. 53-57)?

c. Are the claims of the text morally plausible (pp. 57-58)?

6. Relate the text or topic to the congregation in a responsible way (hermeneutics) (pp. 60-62):

    a. In the case of a sermon or biblical text that is appropriate to the gospel, intelligible, and morally plausible (or mostly so), can you find an illuminating analogy between the situation of the text and the situation today, taking into account both differences and similarities? If you cannot identify an analogy, can you otherwise posit an adequate relationship between the text and the congregation (pp. 62-67)?

    b. In the case of the topical sermon, summarize your theological interpretation of the topic (pp. 67-69).

7. Name how your interpretation of the text or topic relates specifically to the context of the congregation, to individuals in the congregation, to the local setting, to the nation, and to the world (pp. 70-85).

8. Taking into account the congregational context, the claims of the text or topic, and your theological reflection, articulate the good news from God that will be the heart of the sermon. Formulate the sermon in a sentence; that is, put the good news of the sermon into a single indicative sentence using the formula on pp. 20-22.

9. Decide which general pattern of movement—selected from stock patterns or your own creation, deductive or inductive—you think will help the congregation follow the sermon (pp. 86-106).

10. Prepare the sermon itself.

    • Generate a beginning that will invite the congregation into the sermon (pp. 100-102; cf. 89-91, 94, 95-96).

    • Order the central part of the sermon (pp. 91-93; cf. 95-96).

    • Sketch an ending that will encourage the congregation to continue reflecting on the sermon after you stop speaking (pp. 103-105; cf. 96).

11. Be sure to include at least one lifelike story that portrays the good news of the sermon (pp. 80-85).

12. Prepare to embody the sermon. Practice. Whether you work with a manuscript or notes, or preach without anything in front of you, make sure the sermon is in your heart (pp. 107-14).

Summary of Questions to Guide Sermon Feedback

The following questions are designed for use in a sermon feedback group. In my preaching classes, before a sermon, I assign each student to listen to the sermon while keeping one of the questions below in mind. After the sermon, each student reports on his or her category. For example, one student listens for the good news in the sermon from the perspective of question 1 below, and reports, "The good news that I heard in this sermon is . . . ." Another student listens for the degree to which the preacher honors the integrity of the text or topic (question 2). Each respondent identifies positive qualities in the sermon and suggests points at which the preacher might want to do things differently. Student respondents report that in the process of listening for specific qualities in the preaching, they learn how to become better and more critical listeners to sermons, and they are also sparked to think about their own preaching. In parentheses, I identify pages in this book that discuss the subject matter that is the focus of the question. While questions 8 through 12 are not discussed in the book, their connection to the main themes of the book is clear.

1. What is the good news from God at the heart of this sermon (pp. 20-22)?

2. Does the sermon honor the integrity and otherness of the biblical passage or the topic on which the sermon is focused? If

so, how? If not, what could the preacher do to increase that dimension (pp. 28-48)?

3. Is the sermon theologically adequate? Are the claims appropriate to the gospel? Intelligible (understandable, consistent with other things Christians say and do, seriously imaginable)? Morally plausible (pp. 49-58)?

4. Does the congregation relate the text or topic to the congregation in a responsible way (pp. 59-69)?

5. What is the significance of the sermon for the congregation? What are the specific points of contact with the local context? Could the preacher bring the sermon more fully into the world of the congregation (pp. 70-85)?

6. Did the sermon move in a way that is easy to follow? Describe the movement of the sermon. Comment on things the preacher did that helped you stay on track with the sermon. Note points at which the sermon was not as clear as it could have been. What might the preacher do differently (pp. 86-106)?

7. Did the preacher embody the sermon in an engaging fashion? Comment on different aspects of embodiment: the sense of spirituality, presence, and tone; the voice, eyes, gestures, and other movements; and pauses (pp. 107-14).

8. At what point did this sermon most connect with you?

9. What, in the sermon, most helped this connection?

10. At what point was the sermon most distant, or otherwise difficult, for you? What made it so?

11. What in the sermon most frustrated the sermon's ability to connect with you?

12. What is the most important thing you want to tell the preacher about this sermon?

Appendix C

Plans for Preaching

From week to week, a minister has four options for selecting a focus for the sermon: preaching from (1) a selected lectionary, (2) a continuous lectionary, (3) a series, or (4) free selection. Preachers and congregations must choose which option to follow for a given season. Even after selecting a plan, the preacher and congregation may depart from it if something happens in the community that calls for immediate theological interpretation that the plan would not provide.

(1) *Selected Lectionary.* The term *lectionary* derives from a Latin word for "read" *(lectio),* and in today's church refers to a table of Scripture passages prescribed for reading in worship. A selected lectionary *(lectio selecta)* is one in which the readings are selected by a committee to coordinate with the Christian Year (or some other organizing principle). The Christian Year organizes time according to the following seasons and days that recall and anticipate the redemption of the world:

- Advent—preparing for the coming of Christ and the completion of redemption.

- Christmas—celebrating the incarnation and its role in redemption.

- Epiphany—celebrating the manifestation of Christ to the Gentiles.

- Lent—preparing to ponder the place of the suffering and death of Christ in the scheme of redemption.

- Easter—celebrating the Resurrection as demonstration of God's will and power to redeem.

- Pentecost—celebrating the presence of the Holy Spirit as agent of redemptive power continuously at work in the world.

- Ordinary Time—reflecting on the significance of the events of redemption for the day-to-day life of the present world.

The most popular lectionary in use in North America, the Revised Common Lectionary (RCL), selects passages from the Bible to illumine the theological themes of these seasons.[1] Strictly speaking, when preaching from the RCL, the preacher does not simply preach the text, but he or she develops the sermon to explore how the text helps the congregation interpret the theological themes of the season in which the text appears. In Advent, for instance, the preacher asks how the Bible readings help him or her prepare for the coming of Christ in glory and the completion of the redemption of the world.

Each Sunday, the RCL prescribes four readings: one from a Gospel, one from a Letter, one from the First Testament (except after Easter when this reading is replaced by one from Acts), and a psalm (which is really for liturgical use, though it can be the focus of the sermon). In the cycles of Advent-Christmas-Epiphany and Lent-Easter-Pentecost, the readings are coordinated with the Gospels setting the main themes for the day, and the other readings supporting those themes. In Ordinary Time, the RCL largely reads continuously through Matthew, Mark, and Luke, and some of the Epistles. During this season, the RCL provides two readings from the First Testament and the psalms: one that coordinates with the Gospels, and one that reads continuously through a section of the First Testament. A preacher must choose which readings from the First Testament to use.

The RCL is divided into three years, each with a focus on a different Gospel. Year A—Matthew; Year B—Mark; Year C—Luke. Readings from the Gospel of John are interspersed.

This approach, like continuous lectionary and sermon series, gives the preacher a place to start sermon preparation each Monday. It keeps several fulcrum doctrines and themes of Christian faith in the consciousness of the congregation. It provides

121

a theological framework within which to interpret the Bible and other dimensions of Christian tradition. It takes the community through several important parts of the Bible, including some texts that pastors and people might otherwise avoid.

However, preaching from a selected lectionary in the context of the Christian Year presents the congregation with only a limited selection of biblical texts and Christian doctrines. Some essential Christian motifs are muted or absent (for example, a sustained consideration of the doctrine of creation). The lectionary contributes to anti-Judaism by subordinating the readings from the First Testament to the gospel. Congregations are often bewildered by the lectionary's assignments for Advent-Christmas-Epiphany and Lent-Easter-Pentecost. I myself weary of hearing the same gospel lections cycle after cycle.

(2) *Continuous Lectionary (lectio continua).* In this plan, the preacher and congregation move passage by passage through a book of the Bible. The preacher, perhaps in conjunction with congregational leaders, determines that the congregation will benefit from hearing a sermon that offers an exposition of a particular book of the Bible, or a part of a book of the Bible. For example, a pastor might preach through Romans or through Isaiah 40–55.

The preacher must divide the book, or other section of the Bible, into passages of meaningful length. While each sermon needs to focus on a meaningful unit, the preacher needs to adjust the total number of sermons to the congregation's attention span. Some communities can follow an exposition of a biblical book for several months, while others tire after six to eight weeks.

The Revised Common Lectionary provides for a version of continuous reading in Ordinary Time. The congregation reads through major sections of the Gospels of Matthew, Mark, and Luke, as well as through the Letters of the Second Testament. The RCL also provides an option for reading continuously through portions of the First Testament.

Preaching from a continuous lectionary gives the preacher a place to start sermon preparation each Monday. It provides continuity from week to week. It introduces the congregation in-depth to a significant piece of the Bible. It can take the congregation in the direction of theological concerns that have a low profile, or do not even appear, in the Christian Year or the Revised Common

Lectionary. However, the weeks of exposition sometimes drag beyond the attention span of the congregation.

(3) *Sermon series.* A preacher can put together a series of sermons that consider a topic, a biblical theme, or some other focus. A preacher might put together a series on the elements of worship, or on a doctrine, a Christian practice, or a theological or ethical matter.

When developing a series, each sermon needs to be connected with the other messages in the sequence and to stand by itself. The latter is important because few listeners hear all the sermons in the series; some members hear only one sermon. That one message needs to be meaningful for them. To help members of the community set individual sermons in the context of the series, the preacher might provide a summary of the sermon series in the worship bulletin and church newsletter, or provide a brief oral outline of the series and its purpose.

The Christian Year is not inherently tied to the lectionary. A preacher could use the theological motifs of a season of the Christian Year to develop a series of topical sermons on those motifs. In Advent, for example, the preacher could put together a series on different ways Christ came to us, comes to us now, and will come.

A series gives the congregation an opportunity to consider a motif in more depth and breadth than is afforded by a single sermon. It allows the preacher to correlate systematically the resources of Christian reflection with the context and needs of the congregation. However, if the subject of the series is not well chosen or well focused, listening to the series can become an experience in frustration and irrelevance for the community.

(4) *Free selection.* From one week to another, the preacher freely selects the subject of the sermon—usually a biblical text or theme, a theological doctrine, a Christian practice, or other topic. The preacher chooses a focal point that will benefit the congregation. Over a series of weeks, the selections may range very widely in focus, or they may share a common concern without being joined together in a series. A preacher often makes selections in accord with the church calendar.

Free selection gives the preacher optimum freedom in choosing the focus of the message. As in developing a series, free selection, allows the preacher to correlate the resources of Christian reflection with the immediate need and situation of the community. However, if the center point of the sermon is not well chosen, the experience of listening to the message can be inconsequential and even annoying. Preachers who habitually use free selection often preach from a very limited selection of texts or topics. They turn again and again to the same biblical books, doctrines, or other concerns, and neglect other materials that are essential for growth in Christian faith and life. Further, preachers who follow this method can easily let the subjects of preaching become captive to calendars and concerns that are peripheral, or even alien, to Christian community.

Appendix D

Resources for Beginning Preachers

This appendix lists and briefly annotates some basic resources for beginning preachers. Persons who are new to preaching could begin by selecting at least one book or journal from each category below. My personal favorites are marked with an asterisk.

Key Journal. *Homiletic* is mainly a review journal. Considers almost all contemporary books on preaching. Keeps one up to date. **Homiletic*, Perkins School of Theology, Southern Methodist University, Dallas, TX 75275 (214-768-2183).

Full-scale Introductions to Preaching. The following books are general introductions to preaching that give more attention to the nuts and bolts of sermon preparation than *Preaching: An Essential Guide:* Ronald J. Allen, *Interpreting the Gospel: An Introduction to Preaching* (St. Louis: Chalice Press, 1998); comprehensive introduction to preaching as conversation with biblical texts, biblical themes, doctrines, Christian practices, and topics. Thomas G. Long, *The Witness of Preaching* (Louisville: Westminster John Knox Press, 1989); luminous introduction to expository preaching.

John S. McClure, ed. *Best Advice for Preaching* (Minneapolis: Fortress Press, 1998); twenty-seven preachers and scholars of preaching comment on aspects of preaching ranging from the call to preach to resources for sermon preparation. Henry Mitchell, *Black Preaching* (Nashville: Abingdon Press, 1990); fundamental introduction to history and practice of African American preaching. Paul

Scott Wilson. *The Four Pages of the Sermon: A Guide to Biblical Preaching*. Nashville: Abingdon Press, 1999; sees sermon in four parts: trouble in text, trouble in our world, grace in text, and grace in our world. Paul Scott Wilson, *The Practice of Preaching* (Nashville: Abingdon Press, 1995); introduction to expository preaching, taking account of orality, rhetoric, hermeneutics, and poetics.

Collections of Sermons. Reading, hearing, and watching other preachers often helps beginning preachers find their own voices: Ronald J. Allen, ed. *Patterns for Preaching: A Sermon Sampler* (St. Louis: Chalice Press, 1998); describes and illustrates thirty-four different ways of preaching; includes racial/ethnic sermons in addition to European American sermons. Mark Barger Elliott, *Creative Styles of Preaching* (Louisville: Westminster John Knox Press, 2000); recent approaches to preaching: narrative, African American, evangelistic, topical, four pages, literary forms, pastoral biblical, and imaginative. Thomas G. Long and Cornelius Plantinga, Jr., eds. *A Chorus of Witnesses: Model Sermons for Today's Preacher* (Grand Rapids: Wm. B. Eerdmans Publishing Co., 1994); example of variety in sources, aims, forms, dynamics, and occasions.

Study Bible. A preacher should have a good study Bible on the desk for immediate help in biblical interpretation: *The HarperCollins Study Bible: New Revised Standard Version, with the Apocryphal/Deuterocanonical Books* (New York: HarperCollins, 1993).

Bible Commentaries. At the start of a preaching ministry, a one-volume commentary is indispensable: *James L. Mays, ed., *Harper's Bible Commentary*, rev. ed. (San Francisco: HarperSanFrancisco, 2000); one of the most widely used one-volume commentaries. Watson Mills and Richard Wilson, eds., *Mercer Bible Commentary* (Macon, Ga.: Mercer University Press, 1995). Cain Hope Felder, ed., *The Original African Heritage Study Bible* (Iowa Falls, Iowa: World Bible Publishers, 1993); highlights African American perspectives in interpretation. Carol Newsom and Sharon Ringe, eds., *Women's Bible Commentary* (Louisville: Westminster John Knox Press, 1998); calls attention to issues related to women in biblical texts. Elisabeth Schüssler Fiorenza, *Searching the Scriptures: A Feminist Commentary* (New York: Crossroad, 1993–94), 2 vols.; brings women's voices to surface as well as tells how women have been silenced.

Preachers should build a library of commentaries on books of the Bible. By purchasing a commentary a month, a preacher can accumulate an excellent collection in a way that is not financially painful. Commentaries are often published in series. Although the quality of individual volumes varies widely within a series, the following series are generally reliable and pitched at a level that beginning preachers can grasp: *Interpretation: A Bible Commentary for Preaching and Teaching* (Louisville: Westminster John Knox Press) and *The New Interpreter's Bible* (Nashville: Abingdon Press).

Bible Dictionaries. A Bible dictionary provides in-depth study of key words in the Bible. A preacher can start with a one-volume dictionary then add multiple-volume dictionaries. David Noel Freedman, ed., *Eerdmans Dictionary of the Bible* (Grand Rapids: Wm. B. Eerdmans Publishing Co., 2000). *James L. Mays, ed., *The HarperCollins Bible Dictionary*, rev. ed. (San Francisco: HarperSanFrancisco, 1996). Watson Mills, ed., *Mercer Dictionary of the Bible* (Macon, Ga.: Mercer University Press, 1990). All provide basic information about the Bible.

Accessible multivolume Bible dictionaries include *George R. Buttrick, ed., *The Interpreter's Dictionary of the Bible* (Nashville: Abingdon Press, 1964, 1975), 5 vols.; as well as David Noel Freedman, ed., *Anchor Bible Dictionary* (New York: Doubleday Publishing Co., 1992), 6 vols. More detailed studies of words, places, books, and so forth.

Dictionaries of Church History. I notice that few preachers' libraries contain dictionaries of church history. However, such works can provide invaluable information on how interpretation of the Bible and Christian theology have evolved over time: *E. A. Livingstone, ed., *The Oxford Dictionary of the Christian Church.* 3d. ed. (York: Oxford University Press, 1997); standard work. Trevor Hart, ed., *The Dictionary of Historical Theology* (Grand Rapids: Wm. B. Eerdmans, 2000); traces classic doctrines through history.

Dictionaries of Theology. A dictionary of theology provides capsules on how the Christian community interprets essential matters in Christian faith and life: *Alan Richardson and John Bowden, *The Westminster Dictionary of Christian Theology* (Philadelphia: The Westminster Press, 1983); excellent summaries of wide range of theological concepts. Donald Musser and Joseph Price, *A New Handbook of Christian Theology* (Nashville: Abingdon Press, 1992); extended discussions of selected motifs. Van A. Harvey, *A Handbook of Theological Terms* (New York: Macmillan Publishing Co., 1964); classic summaries of theological views into the 1960s; still in print.

Commentaries on the Revised Common Lectionary. The following are Bible commentaries (with suggestions for preaching) on texts in the Revised Common Lectionary: Walter Brueggemann, Charles Cousar, Beverly Roberts Gaventa, and James Newsome, *Texts for Preaching: A Lectionary Commentary Based on the New Revised Lectionary* (Louisville: Westminster John Knox Press, 1992–94), 3 vols. *Shelley E. Cochran, *The Pastor's Underground Guide to the Revised Common Lectionary* (St. Louis: Chalice Press, 1995–97), 3 vols. Fred Craddock, John Hayes, Carl Holladay, and Gene Tucker, *Preaching Through the Christian Year: A Comprehensive Commentary on the Lectionary* (Philadelphia: Trinity Press International, 1992–94), 3 vols. Marion Soards, Thomas Dozeman, and Kendall McCabe, *Preaching the Revised Common Lectionary* (Nashville: Abingdon Press, 1992–94), 3 vols.

Journals of Sermon Helps. Many journals provide help for the lectionary preacher. Three that I find especially useful: *Biblical Preaching Journal* provides an exegesis and a sermon for one text for each Sunday of the Christian Year; P.O. Box 503, Versailles, KY 40383-0503 (859-873-0550). *Lectionary Homiletics* offers an exegesis for every Sunday of the year, along with theological and pastoral comments, the appearance of the text in the arts; reviews of other sermons on the text, and suggestions for preaching; 13540 E. Boundary Road, Suite 105B, Midlothian, VA 23112-3943 (800-866-8631). *Preaching: Word and Witness* contains an exegesis, suggestions for the service of worship, stories, and a sample sermon; Liturgical Publications, 2875 S. James Drive, New Berlin, WI, 53151 (262-785-1188).

Two journals are especially helpful for preaching from individual texts (free selection) that are not in the lectionary or from biblical themes: *Preaching Great Texts: The Unlectionary Journal* contains notes toward sermons, and responses to the sermon (by someone other than the preacher) on a wide variety of texts; 13540

E. Boundary Road, Suite 105B, Midlothian, VA 23112-3943 (800-866-8631). Each issue of *The Living Pulpit* centers on a particular theological theme, with interpretive articles from the Bible, church history, theology, and contemporary reflections; 5000 Independence Avenue, Bronx, NY 10471 (718-542-6113).

NOTES

Introduction

1. Along this line, I avoid the term *homiletics*. Pastors and scholars typically use this word as a synonym for *preaching*, though some people employ it as a specialized term for the academic discipline that studies preaching. I avoid *homiletics* because it is unfamiliar to most congregations. Preachers should keep the language of preaching as close as possible to the everyday language spoken in a congregation.

Sample Sermon

1. "How Firm a Foundation," *Chalice Hymnal* (St. Louis: Chalice Press, 1995), no. 618.

1. What Is the Good News from God in the Sermon?

1. For an overview of different ways of understanding the purpose of preaching, and the functions of various participants in the event of preaching, see Richard Lischer, *Theories of Preaching: Selected Readings in the Homiletical Tradition* (Durham: The Labyrinth Press, 1987), and Eugene L. Lowry, *The Sermon: Dancing the Edge of Mystery* (Nashville: Abingdon Press, 1997).

2. For a fuller discussion of this conviction, see Ronald J. Allen, *Preaching for Growth* (St. Louis: CBP Press, 1987), and idem, with Clark M. Williamson, *A Credible and Timely Word: Process Theology and Preaching* (St. Louis: Chalice Press, 1991), passim. For a similar approach, see Paul Scott Wilson, *The Practice of Preaching* (Nashville: Abingdon Press, 1995), 98-124.

3. For a summary of other ways of focusing the sermon, see Wilson, *The Practice of Preaching*, 152-54.

4. For discussion, see Robert Reid, Jeffrey Bullock, and David Fleer, "Preaching as the Creation of an Experience: The Not-So-Rational Revolution of the New Homiletic," *The Journal of Communication and Religion* 18/1 (1995): 1-18.

5. Ronald J. Allen, ed., *Patterns of Preaching: A Sermon Sampler* (St. Louis: Chalice Press, 1998).

6. This section of the chapter is based on my own theology of preaching, developed more fully in Clark M. Williamson and Ronald J. Allen, *Adventures of the Spirit: A Guide to Worship from the Perspective of Process Theology* (Lanham, Md.: University Press of America, 1997), 137-58; as well as Ronald J. Allen, Barbara Shires Blaisdell, and Scott Black Johnson, *Theology for Preaching: Authority, Truth, and Knowledge of God in a Postmodern Ethos* (Nashville: Abingdon Press, 1997), 111-36. Lischer, *Theories of Preaching*, overviews several key theologies of preaching. For a fascinating delineation of the relationship between particular theological viewpoints and preaching, see Donald K. McKim, *The Bible in Theology and Preaching: A Theological Guide for Preaching* (Nashville: Abingdon Press, 1993).

7. When persons, congregations, or other communities continually refuse the possibilities for restoration that God places before them, and make a life of idolatry, racism, sexism, exploitation, violence, and other forms of sin, these things set in motion forces that lead to personal and corporate collapse.

2. Does the Sermon Honor the Integrity of the Bible or the Topic?

1. For further discussion of the integrity of the text or topic, see Clark M. Williamson and Ronald J. Allen, *Adventures of the Spirit: A Guide to Worship from the Perspective of Process Theology* (Lanham, Md.: University Press of America, 1997), 113-36.

2. Ronald J. Allen, "Preaching and Postmodernism," *Interpretation* 55 (2001): 40-42; idem, "Preaching and the Other," *Worship* 76 (2002): 211-24.

3. For overviews of various exegetical methods, see Ronald J. Allen, *Contemporary Biblical Interpretation for Preaching* (Valley Forge: Judson Press, 1984); Stephen V. Farris, *Preaching That Matters: The Bible and Our Lives* (Louisville: Westminster John Knox Press, 1998), 39-74; David L. Bartlett, *Between the Bible and the Church: New Methods for Biblical Preaching* (Nashville: Abingdon Press, 1999); Steven L. McKenzie and Stephen R. Haynes, eds., *To Each Its Own: An Introduction to Biblical Criticisms and Their Applications* (Louisville: Westminster John Knox Press, 1999).

4. The term *fire* appears in 14:54 when Jesus is on trial and Peter is warming himself by the fire outside the house of the high priest immediately prior to denying Jesus. This event is a kind of tribulation fire, but it is not clear that the tribulation fire is really in the background of 14:54.

5. On topical preaching, see Ronald J. Allen, *Preaching the Topical Sermon* (Louisville: Westminster John Knox Press, 1992); idem, *Interpreting the Gospel: An Introduction to Preaching* (St. Louis: Chalice Press, 1998), as well as Jane Rzepka and Ken Sawyer, *Thematic Preaching: An Introduction* (St. Louis: Chalice Press, 2001).

6. Paul Scott Wilson, *Imagination of the Heart: New Understandings in Preaching* (Nashville: Abingdon Press, 1988), 54-56.

7. For more detailed steps of preparation, see Allen, *Preaching the Topical Sermon*, 37-71.

8. The preacher can often get help in understanding the biblical and historical

backgrounds of a topic from the good Bible dictionaries and dictionaries of Christian history and theology. I have seldom found topical concordances or indexes of the Bible to provide reliable guidance. Often the texts in these latter books are arranged according to nothing more than catchwords.

9. On the characteristics of these theological families, see Allen, *Interpreting the Gospel*, 73-81. For a wider survey, see David F. Ford, *The Modern Theologians: An Introduction to Theology in the Twentieth Century* (Cambridge, Mass.: Blackwell Publishing Co., 1997).

3. Is the Sermon Theologically Adequate?

1. For theological methods, see James O. Duke and Howard W. Stone, *How to Think Theologically?* (Minneapolis: Fortress Press, 1996); Donald G. Luck, *Why Study Theology?* (St. Louis: Chalice Press, 1999).

2. For this method, see Clark M. Williamson and Ronald J. Allen, *The Teaching Minister* (Louisville: Westminster John Knox Press, 1991), 71-129; idem, *A Credible and Timely Word: Process Theology and Preaching* (St. Louis: Chalice Press, 1991), 65-82; Clark M. Williamson, *A Guest in the House of Israel: Post-Holocaust Church Theology* (Louisville: Westminster John Knox Press, 1993), 18-25; idem, *Way of Blessing, Way of Life: A Christian Theology* (St. Louis: Chalice Press, 1999), 29-37; and Ronald J. Allen, *Interpreting the Gospel: An Introduction to Preaching* (St. Louis: Chalice Press, 1998), 65-95.

3. On adequacy as a criterion for theological statements, see David Tracy, *Blessed Rage for Order: The New Pluralism in Theology* (Minneapolis: The Winston Seabury Press, 1975), 70-72.

4. Clark M. Williamson, "Preaching the Gospel: Some Theological Reflections," *Encounter* 49 (1988): 191.

5. The language "seriously imaginable" is from Yale theologian David H. Kelsey, *Proving Doctrine: The Uses of Scripture in Modern Theology* (Harrisburg: Trinity Press International, 1999, o.p. 1975), 170-74.

6. On the transition from the modern to the postmodern worlds, a basic guide is Allen, Blaisdell, and Johnston, *Theology for Preaching*.

4. Does the Sermon Relate the Text or Topic to the Congregation in a Responsible Way?

1. In many other disciplines (for example, literary theory), the term *hermeneutics* often refers to all aspects of the interpretation of a text. However, in preaching, hermeneutics refers more narrowly to the process whereby the preacher moves from the meaning of a text in the past to its meaning in the present.

2. The best guide to the hermeneutic of analogy is Stephen Farris, *Preaching That Matters: The Bible and Our Lives* (Louisville: Westminster John Knox Press, 1998), esp. 74-124. The work of James A. Sanders is pivotal, for example, his *Canon and Community: A Guide to Canonical Criticism*, Guides to Biblical Scholarship (Philadelphia: Fortress Press, 1984), 46-60.

3. Farris, *Preaching That Matters*, 77.

4. Ibid., 77-80.

5. What Is the Significance of the Sermon for the Congregation?

1. The following books are essential reading for these tasks: Leonora Tubbs Tisdale, *Preaching as Local Theology and Folk Art*, Fortress Resources for Preaching (Minneapolis: Fortress Press, 1997); Nancy T. Ammerman, Jackson W. Carroll, Carl S. Dudley, and William McKinney, eds., *Studying Congregations: A New Handbook* (Nashville: Abingdon Press, 1998); Stephen Farris, *Preaching That Matters: The Bible and Our Lives* (Louisville: Westminster John Knox Press, 1998), esp. 30-38; Thomas Edward Frank, *The Soul of the Congregation: An Invitation to Congregational Reflection* (Nashville: Abingdon Press, 2000); and James R. Neiman and Thomas G. Rodgers, *Preaching from Pew to Pew* (Minneapolis: Fortress Press, 2001). The preacher can further employ listening skills learned in pastoral counseling, and modes of theological and social analysis from systematic theology, ethics, sociology of religion.

2. George Parsons and Speed Leas, *Understanding Your Congregation as a System* (Washington, D.C.: Alban Institute, 1993), 9.

3. On listening skills, a helpful guide is John Savage, *Listening and Caring Skills: A Guide for Group Leaders* (Nashville: Abingdon Press, 1996).

4. John S. McClure, *The Round Table Pulpit: Where People and Leadership Meet* (Nashville: Abingdon Press, 1995).

5. For further discussion on this theme, see Joseph R. Jeter, Jr., and Ronald J. Allen, *One Gospel, Many Ears: Preaching to Different Listeners in the Congregation* (St. Louis: Chalice Press, 2002).

6. For a discussion on preaching as a guest, see Ronald J. Allen, "The One-Shot Preaching Assignment," *Preaching* 7/2 (1991): 41-46.

7. Farris, *Preaching That Matters*, 33-38.

8. For a popular summary of these developments, see Allen, Blaisdell, and Johnston, *Theology for Preaching*, 87-111.

9. David G. Buttrick, *Homiletic: Moves and Structures* (Philadelphia: Fortress Press, 1987), 141-43.

10. As representative of this material, see Richard Thulin, *The "I" of the Sermon: Autobiography in the Pulpit*, Fortress Resources for Preaching (Minneapolis: Fortress Press, 1989).

6. Does the Sermon Move in a Way That Is Easy to Follow?

1. I borrow the notion of the stockroom from Thomas G. Long, *The Witness of Preaching* (Louisville: Westminster John Knox Press, 1989), 126-29.

2. Allen, *Patterns of Preaching*.

3. From Ronald J. Allen, "The Sermon," in *Preaching: Word and Witness* 1/1 (2000).

4. On this approach to preaching, see Allen, *Patterns of Preaching*, 22-28.

5. Long, *The Witness of Preaching*, 94-95.

6. Ronald J. Allen, "Why We Can Believe in God Today" in Allen, Blaisdell, and Johnston, *Theology for Preaching*, 204-13.

7. See Allen, *Patterns of Preaching*, 64-71.

8. Craddock, *As One Without Authority*, 99-100.

9. Ronald J. Allen, *The Teaching Sermon* (Nashville: Abingdon Press, 1995), 95-102.

10. Cf. Allen, *Patterns of Preaching*, 131-37; idem, *The Teaching Sermon*, 109-16.

11. From a sermon preached at First Christian Church, Omaha, Nebraska. Used by permission.

12. From a sermon preached at Tustin Presbyterian Church, Tustin, California. Used by permission.

13. Barbara Brown Taylor, *God in Pain: Teaching Sermons on Suffering*. The Teaching Sermon Series (Nashville: Abingdon Press, 1998), 27.

14. From a sermon preached at Tustin Presbyterian Church, Tustin, California. Used by permission.

15. Brown Taylor, *God in Pain*, 40.

16. Marjorie Hewitt Suchocki, *The Whispered Word: A Theology of Preaching* (St. Louis: Chalice Press, 1999), 114.

7. Does the Preacher Embody the Sermon in an Engaging Way?

1. See Joseph M. Webb, *Preaching Without Notes* (Nashville: Abingdon Press, 2000).

Appendix C

1. For the readings, see "The Consultation on Common Texts," *The Revised Common Lectionary* (Nashville: Abingdon Press, 1992).

DATE DUE

HIGHSMITH #45230

Printed
in USA